DATE DUE

APR 1 3 2017	

REAGAN'S COMEBACK

REAGAN'S COMEBACK

FOUR WEEKS IN TEXAS THAT CHANGED
AMERICAN POLITICS FOREVER

GILBERT GARCIA

TRINITY UNIVERSITY PRESS
SAN ANTONIO

Published by Trinity University Press
San Antonio, Texas 78212
Copyright © 2012 by Gilbert Garcia

Cover design by Anne Richmond, Boston
Book design by BookMatters, Berkeley

Trinity University Press strives to produce its books using methods and materials in an environmentally sensitive manner. We favor working with manufacturers that practice sustainable management of all natural resources, produce paper using recycled stock, and manage forests with the best possible practices for people, biodiversity, and sustainability. The press is a member of the Green Press Initiative, a nonprofit program dedicated to supporting publishers in their efforts to reduce their impacts on endangered forests, climate change, and forest dependent communities.

The paper used in this publication meets the minimum requirements of the American National Standard for Information Sciences—Permanence of Paper for Printed Library Materials, ANSI 39.48-1992.

Library of Congress Cataloging-in-Publication Data

Garcia, Gilbert.
Reagan's comeback : four weeks in Texas that changed American politics forever / Gilbert Garcia.
    p.   cm.
  Includes bibliographical references and index.
  ISBN 978-1-59534-115-0 (hardcover : alk. paper)
  1. Presidents—United States—Election—1976. 2. United States—Politics and government—1974–1977. 3. Reagan, Ronald. 4. Political campaigns—United States—History—20th century. 5. Presidential candidates—United States—Biography. 6. Presidents—United States—Biography. I. Title.
E868.G37 2012
973.927—dc23   2011036600

16   15   14   13   12   5   4   3   2   1

CONTENTS

 # INTRODUCTION

Steve Bartlett had always been a loyal Republican foot soldier. In 1964, as a ruddy-faced sixteen-year-old Barry Goldwater worshipper, Bartlett formed the first Young Republicans club in Oak Cliff, a historic, middle-class community separated from downtown Dallas by the Trinity River. He and his fellow teen conservatives were so enthralled with Goldwater's quixotic presidential bid that they showed up at Kimball High School the day after the November election wearing tie tags adorned with the number "27," just to inform the nonbelievers that their man had received 27 million votes (never mind the fact that his Democratic opponent, Lyndon Johnson, had garnered more than 43 million).

Bartlett, who would go on to become a four-term North Texas congressman and the mayor of Dallas, was so determined to spread the good word of Republicanism that in 1974, with his party reeling from the Watergate scandal that brought down Richard Nixon's presidency, he revived the dormant Dallas Republican Men's Club "as a dare, to see if there were still Republicans around after Watergate." Bartlett made a habit of doing whatever his party asked, so in 1976, when his state's GOP leaders overwhelmingly backed President Gerald Ford against the intraparty challenge of former California governor Ronald Reagan, Bartlett didn't question it. He fell in line.

In fact, Bartlett was not merely a Ford *supporter*. In a quirk of the newly created Texas presidential primary system, he was a ballot surrogate for the president: one of four Ford delegates from Bartlett's congressional district who appeared on the primary ballot opposite four local Reagan loyalists. So on May 1, 1976, when Reagan handed Ford the most shocking, embarrassing, and lopsided primary defeat ever inflicted on an incumbent American president, Bartlett couldn't help but take it personally.

That night he rolled the results around in his mind. Reagan had won by a 2–1 margin, handily taking every district in the state and claiming all ninety-six contested delegates. (A month later, at the Republican State Convention, he would also collect all four of the state's at-large delegates.) He'd executed this rout despite the fact that Ford had the enthusiastic endorsement of US senator John Tower, the only statewide-elected Republican most Texans had ever known, as well as the more subtle backing of the state's party organization. Ford had more money, he had the power of incumbency, and he went into Texas having dominated his early primary contests with Reagan.

Bartlett couldn't figure out what had gone wrong. He'd taken his delegate role seriously, knocking on doors and calling party regulars. He jokingly blamed his wife, who'd developed a personal affection for Ford, for getting him into this mess. "I remember thinking," he says, "that something is going on that I just don't get."

If the 1976 Texas primary left Bartlett feeling like a cross between Thomas E. Dewey and Bob Dylan's clueless Mr. Jones, he had plenty of company. *Time* magazine responded to the results by trumpeting "Reagan's Startling Texas Landslide,"[1] and political prognosticators around the country tried to explain how a contest widely seen as a toss-up had veered so far off the predicted course.

Neither Bartlett nor the bevy of political reporters on the campaign trail could have known it at the time, but Texas was a pivotal primary, a political watershed that not only salvaged Reagan's political fortunes but helped to reshape the American electoral map.

Because Reagan ultimately lost the 1976 Republican nomination to Ford, the '76 campaign is often shortchanged in his biography. When it *is* analyzed, most attention tends to focus on North Carolina, Reagan's first victory, the primary that punctured Ford's growing aura of inevitability. At least two conservative champions, M. Stanton Evans—one of the few people to land on Nixon's enemies list by attacking him from the right—and Craig Shirley—whose book *Reagan's Revolution: The Untold Story of the Campaign That Started It All* examined the '76 race—have called North Carolina one of the two most important primaries in the history of the American conservative movement (along with Goldwater's 1964 California win).

Coming after five straight early losses to Ford, North Carolina was a much-needed psychological boost for the Reagan campaign. It energized his forces and temporarily quieted talk that their man was about to pull out of the race. In terms of the pure calculus of the race, however, it amounted to little more than a short-term reprieve.

Given the circumstances, Reagan's solid but narrow (52–46 percent) North Carolina win should have been expected. Reagan had spent twelve days campaigning in the state to only two for Ford, and Reagan had the backing of the state's most powerful Republican, US senator Jesse Helms, who turned the primary into a referendum on his own popularity. North Carolina surprised people only because Reagan's early failures had drastically lowered expectations for his campaign. For all the giddiness in the Reagan camp over the North Carolina victory, when the dust cleared from that primary, Reagan had gained a whopping two delegates on Ford.

When Ford rebounded from North Carolina with easy, barely contested wins in Wisconsin, New York, and Pennsylvania, his national delegate lead swelled to the point of being prohibitive. Reagan campaign manager John Sears publicly conceded what everyone knew: If Reagan lost Texas, any hope for the nomination was gone.

North Carolina merely kept Reagan's slim hopes alive until Texas. But Texas made the Ford-Reagan battle a horse race, ensuring that Reagan's campaign would be a force all the way to the national convention three and a half months later in Kansas City. When Ford lost North Carolina, his campaign leaders were annoyed, because they thought complacency had cost them a winnable primary. But they weren't worried. After Ford was drubbed in Texas, however, they knew they were in a dogfight.

If Reagan had fallen short in Texas, he would have emerged from '76 as the man who challenged an accidental president and bombed out in spectacular fashion. Even in 1976, his age (sixty-five) was an issue. By 1980, he would be older than any man who'd ever been elected to the office. Trying to overcome that handicap after failing dismally in '76 probably would have been too much for him. Given the odds, he might have spared himself the ordeal altogether, in favor of riding horses at his California ranch, accepting the occasional speaking engagement, and maintaining his popular syndicated radio commentaries and newspaper columns.

Texas put Reagan in perfect position for 1980 because it enabled him to carry his '76 campaign all the way to the convention, build a national grassroots base, and essentially mold the party platform in his own conservative image. By the time Ford sealed a narrow, 117-delegate victory on the first ballot in Kansas City, Reagan's conservative movement had captured the hearts of the party's rank and file.

Indirectly, the Texas primary also set the stage for one of Reagan's most iconic moments. Because Reagan pushed Ford to the brink of defeat in Kansas City, the president—in the interest of party unity—felt compelled to follow his acceptance speech by inviting Reagan up to the platform to address the convention. Reagan's brief, impromptu speech, about a letter he'd been asked to write for a time capsule that would be opened in one hundred years, reduced grown conservative men to tears. It also left some Ford delegates wondering whether they'd voted for the wrong man.

At the end of that speech, Ray Barnhart, Reagan's brash Texas campaign manager, stared at the podium from his spot near the back of the convention floor and became convinced that his candidate would be back in four years. "Fate had it that he would run again and be elected," Barnhart says.

The Texas primary was also the first demonstration of what came to be known as the Reagan Democrat phenomenon. Texas, unlike most of the early primary states, had an open primary system that allowed people to vote in the contest of their choosing, regardless of their party affiliation. As a result, conservative Democrats—George Wallace Democrats—crossed over in droves for Reagan, and many of them never crossed back.

Reagan actively courted disaffected Democrats in Texas, and after his primary triumph, that phenomenon became a key component of his political formula. Because of the excitement he stirred, the '76 Texas Republican primary attracted nearly 420,000 voters, more than three times the previous state record for a GOP primary.

"Without question, Reagan would have never been president if he hadn't carried Texas 100 percent," says Ernest Angelo, former mayor of the oil-rich West Texas city of Midland, and cochair of Reagan's 1976 Texas campaign. "If he had gotten 65 percent of the delegates it would have been inconsequential, but the fact that he got every delegate and carried every county was a huge loss for Ford. It set Reagan up to be the front-runner for '80, and that wouldn't have happened otherwise."

Steve Munisteri, the current chairman of the Texas Republican Party, was an eighteen-year-old volunteer at Reagan's Houston campaign headquarters in 1976, and he's similarly insistent that Texas was pivotal for Reagan and the American conservative movement. "I've long told people in the Republican National Committee that if it wasn't for Ray Barnhart and Ernie Angelo in '76, there would not be a President Reagan," Munisteri says. "He wasn't even considered a serious candidate when he came down to Texas."

Going into 1976, the spoils of Texas politics were essentially divided between two competing groups: conservative Democrats and liberal Democrats. Republicans barely even factored into the conversation. To put things in perspective, in 1974, only two years before the Reagan-Ford clash, the Texas Democratic primary attracted 1.5 million voters, while the GOP primary drew only 69,000—an astonishing ratio of twenty-two to one. In 1976, the Texas legislature consisted of 160 Democrats and 21 Republicans. Most Texas Republicans simply dreamed of someday having functional voting machines for their all-but-neglected primaries and maybe contesting a few down-ballot judicial races from time to time.

Reagan's triumph changed everything. Above all, it signaled the beginning of a major political realignment—in Texas, the Deep South, and, by extension, the nation as a whole. On the day of the 1976 Texas primary, the GOP held only 16 out of 66 congressional seats from the Deep South. Today, they have 49 out of 69. If you include Texas and Florida in the equation, the Republican Party has gained 66 congressional seats in the South during this period, while the Democratic Party has lost 45.

Two years after Reagan's primary breakthrough, Bill Clements became the first Republican in more than one hundred years to be elected governor of Texas. Over the next several years, many prominent conservative Democrats, derisively dubbed "boll weevils" by their fellow party members, switched to the GOP.

One of these figures, a state legislator from the tiny West Texas ranching community of Paint Creek, would ultimately become the state's longest-serving governor. Rick Perry, like most GOP converts, has credited Reagan with inspiring his switch. Perry is a deeply polarizing figure in his home state, lauded by admirers as "Reagan with a twang" and derided by detractors as a shallow opportunist with a thick head of hair and a thin comprehension of policy nuances. In February 2011, he was one of only two governors in the country to attend the Reagan centennial celebration in Simi Valley, California (even skipping out on a Super Bowl in Arlington, Texas, that same day). He rarely gets through a major speech without invoking Reagan's example and even launched an essay contest in which Texas high schoolers competed for a trip to Washington, DC (or "Devil's City," as Perry jokingly calls it), by writing about Reagan's impact on their lives.

During the 1976 primary campaign, Perry was not yet an active player in Texas politics. He was serving in the US Air Force, flying mammoth C-130 planes all over the globe. A Democrat by birth, and a conservative by nature, he came to politics late, so his reaction to Reagan was a delayed one. In 2010, Perry described his mid-'80s political epiphany this way to *Politics Daily*: "I'm watching Ronald Reagan on television, my dad and I are sitting there saying, 'You know, this guy represents what we believe in.'"[2]

Here's what the Reagan realignment has wrought in Perry's state: No Democratic presidential nominee has carried Texas since 1976; all twenty-nine of its statewide elected offices are currently held by Republicans. And after the Tea Party–fueled GOP surge of 2010, the Republican Party now holds 101 of 150 seats in the Texas House of Representatives.

As Texas has shifted, in the span of thirty years, from one of the country's biggest Democratic strongholds to one of its most rock-solid Republican states, the national impact has been dramatic. Before 1976, not a single Texan had ever sought the Republican presidential nomination—hardly a surprise, given that few GOP politicians in the state even managed to scale the heights of the Texas legislature.

Since 1976, six Texans have sought the Republican presidential nomination, and two have made it to the White House. (In addition, Texas billionaire Ross Perot, a conservative with Republican leanings, received nearly 20 million votes in 1992 as an independent presidential candidate.) In fact, with the exception of 1984 (when Reagan ran for reelection), every post-1976 presidential campaign has included at least one Texas Republican candidate.

Without Reagan's 1976 Texas blowout, the American conservative movement would have lacked a catalyst, a unifying force. The Texas Republican Party, long viewed as an elitist millionaires' club, might still be searching for a populist message. "Until Ronald Reagan came along in 1976 to challenge President Gerald Ford, the GOP in Texas had typically been run by rich folks from Dallas and Houston," wrote Paul Burka in the February 2010 issue of *Texas Monthly*. "The struggle between the GOP establishment and the more conservative populists has been a major theme of Republican politics ever since."[3]

The '76 Ford-Reagan battle was not only an incubator for this new strain of populist conservatism; it was also a bitter tug-of-war for the soul of the GOP. While most Ford supporters now acknowledge Reagan's stature in the party, there remains a tinge of frustration. All those primary voters who showed up for Reagan, they'll tell you, were not "real Republicans." They were not people who had ever shown up for precinct meetings or state conventions. While the point is factually correct, it misses the broader point: Those Reagan 76ers *became* the Republican Party, and all wavering moderates had to either get on Reagan's conservative bus or leave the party.

That rift between hard-core right-wing insurgents and the pragmatic, deal-making party establishment foreshadowed the current tension between the Tea Party movement and so-called RINOs (Republicans in Name Only), who view each other with suspicion and privately expect each other to be the cause of the party's destruction.

Reagan was the undisputed leader of the insurgents in 1976. As many political analysts have suggested, however, the Reagan whose presidency resulted in a tripling of the federal debt, who agreed—albeit grudgingly—to multiple federal tax increases, and who negotiated a sweeping arms-control treaty with the "evil empire" of the Soviet Union (prompting Conservative Caucus leader Howard Phillips to brand him a "useful idiot for Soviet propaganda")[4] would probably not be sufficiently conservative to please today's Tea Party activists.

But that fact only highlights how much Reagan changed the national conversation, how far he moved the goal posts of American politics in ways that his detractors view as odious and his loyalists consider heroic. "In the old days, you used to go to a precinct, state, or national convention, and all the Republicans would fight over abortion," says Mark Elam, a University of Texas freshman who volunteered for Reagan's '76 campaign and later went on to work as US representative Ron Paul's campaign manager. "We don't do that anymore. The pro-life folks totally control the party at the local and national levels. Reagan proved that you could be a true conservative and win."

This is the story of four weeks in the spring of 1976 when Reagan began proving that point, with the help of an army of political misfits and noisy malcontents. It would take Steve Bartlett and others a few years to make sense of it, but the warning shot had been fired.

Author's note: The quotes cited in the notes are from newspapers, magazines, books, and presidential archives. All other quotes are from interviews conducted by the author or televised broadcasts of political speeches.

CHAPTER 1

TEXAS OR BUST

Until February 1976, Ronald Reagan had lived a charmed political life. After a short Depression-era stint as a radio sports announcer in Des Moines, Iowa, he built a three-decade career as a journeyman Hollywood actor, generally playing some variation on the amiable guy next door. A New Deal Democrat for much of his adult life, he steadily developed, over the course of six years as president of the Screen Actors Guild and a stint as a traveling corporate pitchman for General Electric, into a fervent—some would say rabid—Cold Warrior and crusader for the virtues of an unfettered, free-market economy. In 1962, with his acting career reduced to thankless, infrequent TV guest spots, Reagan officially joined the Republican Party.

His ideological transformation may have been gradual, but it was breathtaking nonetheless. The same man who had ardently supported Franklin Roosevelt would ultimately dismiss his former hero by telling *Time* magazine in 1976: "Fascism was really the basis for the New Deal."

In politics, everything seemed to happen so easily for Reagan. Where other political aspirants paid their dues, dutifully collected IOUs, and slowly climbed the electoral-office ladder, Reagan—aided by the residue of goodwill from his long showbiz career—effortlessly sauntered onto the stage and skipped the first few rungs. In 1964, with Barry Goldwater's presidential bid headed for a colossal defeat, Reagan provided the floundering campaign with its one unmistakable spark. His thirty-minute commercial address, which aired nationally on October 27, 1964, was called "A Time for Choosing," but among Reagan supporters it became known simply as "The Speech."

It's remarkable to find, when talking to members of Reagan's '76 campaign team, how many of them trace their devotion to the man back to the exact same moment: the night they tuned in to see him make that speech for Goldwater. M. Stanton Evans, who would later become chairman of the American Conservative Union, remembers turning to his wife after watching the speech and saying, "That's the guy who should be running for president."

Reagan's stump speech for Goldwater was essentially a prime-time infomercial for a pre-infomercial age, but Reagan used it to confidently lay out the broad themes that would constitute the conservative playbook for the next generation: government should be beholden to the people, not the other way around; arrogant elitists in Washington, DC, are determined to "trade our freedom for the soup kitchen of the welfare state"; liberal appeasers are so determined to avoid war that they'll tolerate any act of aggression from the Soviet Union.

After the '64 election, a group of wealthy California business-men who'd supported Goldwater talked Reagan into running for governor of California in 1966. Widely mocked for even pondering a gubernatorial campaign with no previous electoral experience, he shocked popular two-term incumbent Edmund "Pat" Brown—who'd become a Democratic hero by trouncing Richard Nixon in the gubernatorial race four years earlier—and won the election by nearly 1 million votes. Brown and his aides had actually hoped that Reagan would be the GOP nominee, because they viewed him as an ill-informed extremist who would alienate Republican moderates.[5] This be-careful-what-you-wish-for episode marked the first, but hardly the last, time that Reagan would be—to borrow a malapropism later coined by one of his spiritual heirs, George W. Bush—"misunderestimated."

Even Reagan's coy, will-he-or-won't-he presidential flirtation in 1968 enhanced his national stock. Although Reagan didn't campaign in any primary states and didn't declare his candidacy until the outset of the Republican National Convention, the huge margin of his favorite-son win in California meant that he actually netted more national primary votes than Nixon, the eventual GOP nominee.

Going into the 1976 presidential campaign, Reagan had never lost an election for which he'd actively campaigned. That changed on February 24, 1976, in New Hampshire, when Ford eked out a dramatic 1,317-vote upset win. Slender as Ford's margin of victory was there, in the game of political expectations, it was huge. Reagan had entered the fray as a star, a proven vote magnet. Ford went into New Hampshire as the well-intentioned bumbler who'd never run for anything outside the narrow confines of Grand Rapids, Michigan. Ford followed up New Hampshire with four consecutive convincing wins, most notably in Florida—a conservative bastion thought to be in Reagan's wheelhouse—and Illinois—the state where Reagan was born and raised.

While Ford's early successes reflected his organizational superiority, they could also be traced to the curious ambivalence that Reagan brought into the race. After Richard Nixon was reelected in 1972, Reagan looked like an obvious bet for the 1976 race. He'd be leaving the California governor's office in January 1975, and would have plenty of time to mobilize a campaign and devote his full attention to it. But Watergate, and all its collateral damage, threw everything out of kilter for 1976. Vice President Spiro Agnew, another likely '76 contender, faced charges related to a kickback scandal during his time in Maryland state politics, and resigned in disgrace in 1973. Ford, the US House minority leader, best known for his presence a decade earlier on the Warren Commission, which investigated the assassination of John F. Kennedy, was picked by Nixon to replace Agnew.

Nixon famously viewed Ford as someone so blatantly ill-equipped for the nation's highest office that he would provide a form of "impeachment insurance" as the Watergate travesty played itself out. While sitting in the Oval Office in the spring of 1974, he reportedly sneered to former New York governor Nelson Rockefeller, "Can you imagine Jerry Ford sitting in this chair?"[6] Ford, after all, was the man Lyndon Johnson cruelly suggested had spent "too much time playing football without a helmet."

When Nixon resigned in August 1974, Ford initially saw his role as that of a humble, almost apolitical statesman trying to heal the nation's collective wounds. Even after a few months in office, he gave little indication that he might seek a full term in 1976. He had good reason to pause before jumping. By the blunt reckoning of his own staffers, Ford was an inept campaigner and a stilted public speaker with a high propensity for mangling English syntax. He also had to contend with stubbornly high inflation—for which his most conspicuous reaction was wearing a WIN (Whip Inflation Now) button on his lapel—and sluggish economic growth, which led to a palpable sense of unease in the country as 1976 approached.

Like Reagan, Ford was a fiscal conservative at heart, a man who believed in a restrained government, low taxes, and personal self-sufficiency. But the motor of the federal government in the mid-'70s was still being fueled by the momentum of Lyndon Johnson's Great Society. Even after voters implicitly rejected Johnson's ambitious programs by electing Nixon in 1968, neither Nixon nor Ford considered dismantling Johnson's handiwork. Unlike Reagan, Ford was no passionate ideologue. He didn't seek to revolutionize the function of government. He simply wanted to hold it in check.

For that reason, Ford was tolerated by most, but embraced by few. Within the Republican Party, his base was a mile wide, but barely an inch deep. The party's ardent right-wingers viewed him as a blandly compromising career politician and regarded détente—the policy of cooperation with the Soviet Union adhered to by Ford and Secretary of State Henry Kissinger—as a fancy word for appeasement. The party's old Northeast liberal wing, which had been fading in power since Barry Goldwater wrested the 1964 presidential nomination from Nelson Rockefeller, didn't hold much enthusiasm for him either, sensing in him a corn-fed Midwestern jock of limited intelligence and vision.

Even Ford's one indisputable asset—the public perception that he was, as the *Houston Chronicle* put it, "a clean and decent man"— took a major hit a month after his inauguration, when he pardoned Nixon for any crimes he may have committed during his time in office. Ford would spend the last thirty-two years of his life insisting that he had not cut a prearranged deal with Nixon, but his mid-'70s detractors were not easily convinced.

Despite all these warning signs, however, by early 1975 Ford began to develop a strategy for the '76 race, all the while looking over his shoulder and hoping that Reagan would resist the temptation to run. For his part, Reagan now found himself in an awkward position. With Nixon out and Ford in, Reagan's presidential prospects depended on his willingness to tangle with a Republican incumbent, no minor consideration for Reagan, who had once coined what he called the Eleventh Commandment: "Thou shall not speak ill of any fellow Republican."

Reagan's California aides enlisted John Sears, a young Washington, DC, lawyer and political hotshot who'd worked on Nixon's successful 1968 campaign, to persuade their man to take the plunge. It wasn't an easy sell. "Sears convinced the rest of us that Ford would be unsuccessful, but Reagan really was reluctant," a Reagan aide told *Washington Post* political reporter Jules Witcover. "He didn't have that burning, that gut desire to be president that Jimmy Carter or Richard Nixon has."[7] Ultimately convinced that Ford was neither a committed conservative nor an electable candidate, Reagan fought through his reluctance and announced his candidacy on November 20, 1975.

While the threat of a Reagan challenge had sent shudders through the White House for months, at least one prominent Republican believed Ford had nothing to worry about. A September 26, 1975, memo from presidential aide Jerry Jones to fellow aide Donald Rumsfeld and Ford's chief of staff, Dick Cheney, reported that Richard Nixon had privately expressed the view "that Reagan is a lightweight and not someone to be considered seriously or feared. . . . He therefore recommends that we take it easy and not build up Reagan in any way through our actions or our words."[8]

Those words sounded fairly prophetic in the early months of 1976, as Reagan consistently failed to find his campaign footing. Either because of an adherence to the Eleventh Commandment, or the false sense that Ford would be easy to beat, he spoke in generalities about the virtues of limited government and pulled his punches against the president. "We [the American Conservative Union] were not real impressed with the way the Reagan campaign was being run," recalls Evans, who openly backed Reagan in the race. "The Reagan campaign was being run as a kind of above-the-battle, don't-get-too-engaged-in-the-issues thing, as if Reagan were already president. We felt there was no way you were going to beat the incumbent president without giving people a reason to vote against the incumbent."

When Reagan did indulge in policy specifics, the results could be disastrous. His New Hampshire campaign was mortally wounded by his suggestion—in a September 1975 speech—that the federal government could save $90 billion a year by shifting responsibility to the states for programs such as Medicaid, welfare, housing, food stamps, and revenue sharing. The obvious, unanswered question was: How would the states cope with these new burdens? The Ford campaign picked up on the $90 billion speech and made it a big issue in New Hampshire, where voters were panicked at the thought that their state taxes would have to go up to absorb a host of expensive federal programs. (Later in the campaign, Reagan scared uncommitted voters in the Deep South by suggesting that he would "look at" the idea of having the government sell the Tennessee Valley Authority to private interests. This gaffe almost certainly cost Reagan the Kentucky primary.)

As the March 23 North Carolina primary approached, Reagan's campaign was nearly $2 million in debt. Nine Republican governors called for him to step aside and help the party unite behind Ford. On March 20, Sears—without Reagan's knowledge—quietly began preparing for that eventuality by meeting with Rogers Morton, Ford's campaign manager, to discuss how the two campaigns could be brought together after Reagan dropped out. Even Reagan's wife, Nancy, had given up hope and begun privately prodding Lyn Nofziger, the campaign's chronically disheveled press secretary, to persuade her husband to quit.

Reagan's surprise win in North Carolina put a temporary halt to all the when-are-you-quitting? questions he'd begun fielding on a daily basis, but his task remained overwhelming, particularly after Sears decided to ration the campaign's negligible resources and concede Wisconsin, New York, and Pennsylvania to Ford. Handing Wisconsin to Ford was particularly painful, because it was the first of the '76 primary states that allowed voters to cross over and vote outside their party. Reagan believed he could lure disgruntled Democrats into his fold, but his aborted campaign in Wisconsin would fail to prove anything.

Coming out of North Carolina, the Ford and Reagan forces agreed on one key point: Everything hinged on Texas. In late March, more than a month before the Texas primary, Sears told *Washington Post* columnist David Broder that "[Reagan] will survive until Texas, but if he doesn't win there, he's out."

An April 7 memo from Ford campaign lieutenant Bruce Wagner to Morton—sensing the chance for a knockout punch—argued for an aggressive, all-out, attack-dog strategy from Ford. "The Texas primary offers us the opportunity to cut the Reagan candidacy down once and for all," Wagner wrote. "He must be stopped in Texas. A loss in Texas will most likely end his challenge. . . . A win in Texas will most likely allow him to go into [the] Kansas City [convention] via California with momentum."[9]

Pat Buchanan, a conservative political columnist who'd served in the Nixon White House, similarly argued that Texas was Reagan's final hope for a beachhead in the campaign. "The importance of the Texas primary is difficult to overestimate," Buchanan wrote. "Texas is the heart of the sunbelt. It is conservative country and Reagan is right on the issues: defense, détente, and energy. If he loses decisively in Texas, he will have no credible claim to the nomination."[10] Privately, Reagan and Sears agreed that anything short of an outright victory in Texas meant that Reagan should drop out of the race.

When Reagan landed in Texas, twenty-six days before the primary that would define his political future, he did so on a commercial flight. On arriving in Dallas, he conceded to reporters that he'd been forced to give up his red, white, and blue private jet in order to save his cash-strapped campaign $50,000 a week in rental expenses.

He would also find himself relying on a zealous but unproven collection of outsiders: Ray Barnhart, a scrappy professional ditch-digger from the Houston suburb of Pasadena, who'd served one stormy term in the Texas House before voters sent him back to private life; Ernest Angelo, a West Texas oilman who'd stumbled into a political career by moonlighting as the mayor of Midland; Barbara Staff, a Dallas GOP women's club member whose chief credential was her membership in the parish of powerhouse Baptist minister (and social conservative extraordinaire) W. A. Criswell; Jimmy Lyon, a perpetually nervous Houston banker entranced but frequently overwhelmed by the world of politics; Rollie Millirons, a George Wallace Democrat from Fort Worth who decided his man had no chance and switched (personal and party) allegiances for Reagan; and Ron Paul, a suburban obstetrician obsessed with the nation's abandonment of the gold standard, who had won election to Congress less than a month before the presidential primary.

Reagan greeted reporters in Dallas that day by announcing that Texas would be an "uphill fight," because most Republican elected officials were lined up against him. He vowed, however, to "fight the Republican hierarchy by taking his case 'to the people,'"[11] as the *Dallas Morning News* reported.

At one point, a reporter asked Reagan how effective his so-called "people's campaign" could realistically hope to be in the state. Reagan's quick retort said nothing and everything at the same time: "You can cross over here, can't you?"

The answer to that question would provide the key to his fading presidential hopes.

CHAPTER 2
FAVOR FOR A FAVORITE SON

Reagan could thank the Democrats of the Texas legislature that he even had a Texas primary in which to wage his last-ditch battle. Prior to 1976, the state had never held a presidential primary, and the issue might not have come up in the '76 election cycle except for the fact that a prominent political figure from the Lone Star State decided he wanted to be president.

In many ways, Lloyd Bentsen was a classic Texas Democrat. A wealthy businessman with rural family roots and Houston investment banking experience, he possessed a courtly Old World demeanor, a lanky Abe Lincoln frame, and a conservative-to-moderate voting record that enabled him to cut across his state's partisan divide. To this day, some Texas Republicans suggest that if he'd been born a generation later, Bentsen might have gravitated to the GOP.

Bentsen's parents were Danish immigrants who settled in South Dakota before opting for the warmer climate of the Rio Grande Valley, a predominantly Latino stretch of small farm towns along the Texas-Mexico border. After graduating from the University of Texas Law School in 1942, he served in the air force during World War II, flying B-24s over Italy and earning a prestigious Distinguished Flying Cross for leading bombing raids over heavily protected Nazi targets. Following a short stint as a county judge in the Valley, he won election to the US House of Representatives in 1948, two years after John F. Kennedy—who would later play a posthumous supporting role in Bentsen's most (only?) memorable career sound bite—was elected to the House from Massachusetts.

At twenty-seven, Bentsen was the youngest member of Congress, and House Speaker Sam Rayburn, the chrome-plated titan of Texas politics, quickly invited him into his exclusive inner circle, where Bentsen joined the likes of Lyndon Johnson—his state's freshman US senator—and President Harry Truman for bourbon-and-gossip bull sessions.[12]

After only three terms in Congress, however, he decided that his congressional salary of $12,500 a year simply didn't cut it, and he ditched his promising political career to launch Consolidated American Life Insurance Company, a venture that grew into an ultra-lucrative Houston financial holding company. For fifteen years, he steered clear of political temptation, save for a brief 1964 flirtation with the US Senate, a bid that he abruptly terminated in January of that year—only a week before his scheduled campaign-kickoff announcement. Bentsen cited "personal and business obligations," but, in truth, his mind was made up for him by Lyndon Johnson. The new president, who had previously been eager to oust eternally embattled progressive senator Ralph Yarborough, struck a peacekeeping bargain with organized labor to protect Yarborough from any serious Democratic opposition. Bentsen had to be sacrificed in the name of party unity.

Going into 1976, Bentsen had only one statewide election on his résumé, but it was a fairly impressive one: In 1970, he knocked off Yarborough in the Democratic primary for the US Senate. That November, he held off a tough general-election challenge from deep-pocketed, well-connected Republican congressman George Bush.

Even with less than a full Senate term—and a fairly quiet one at that—under his belt, Bentsen decided to compete for the 1976 Democratic presidential nomination. Though hardly a nationally recognized name, he had reason for early optimism. Coming off the Democrats' presidential-campaign debacle of '72, in which liberal favorite George McGovern lost forty-nine of fifty states to Nixon, many party leaders sensed the need for a more moderate figure who could repair the growing cracks in what had formerly been the Solid South. Bentsen seemed to fit the party's new model for success. In 1974, before Bentsen had even officially declared for the presidency, famed oddsmaker Jimmy "The Greek" Snyder—a man better known for his football betting lines than his political acumen—made him a respectable 4:1 shot for the Democratic nomination.

In late 1974, Bentsen's campaign committee paid nearly $13,000 on a private poll meant to gauge whether Texans supported the concept of a presidential primary in the state. The poll found that 67 percent of Texas voters liked the idea. During this same period, Bentsen consulted with Democratic state legislators and encouraged them to use their 1975 session to pass a presidential-primary bill.

On February 17, 1975, Bentsen officially announced his candidacy. Exactly a week before that announcement, state representative Tom Schieffer introduced a bill in the Texas House calling for the creation of a state presidential primary. Schieffer's legislation was a transparent attempt to boost Bentsen's presidential hopes by setting him up for a big win in his home state. In fact, the effort was so transparent that it came to be known among reporters around the Pink Dome (the nickname for the state capitol) as the Bentsen Primary Bill.

The primary rules established by the law were custom-made

for the Texas senator. Each presidential candidate would have a slate of delegates, selected by a committee appointed by that candidate, representing them on the ballot in each district. Someone wanting to cast a primary vote for Bentsen would actually vote for four Bentsen delegates named on the ballot. Given Bentsen's big-name political connections in the state, this format gave him a huge advantage.

Bentsen's opponents would have to scramble to find reasonably prominent Texans to stand in for them on the ballot, while Bentsen would have all the coveted Democratic vote magnets safely in his column. Sure enough, his expertly assembled, big-tent delegate slate ultimately included a veritable rainbow coalition of Latinos (Bexar County Commissioner Albert Bustamante), African Americans (state representatives Anthony Hall, Senfronia Thompson, Eddie Bernice Johnson, and G. J. Sutton), women (former Democratic Party National Committeewoman Carrin Patman), labor leaders, and business titans.

Schieffer's bill also set up an audacious winner-take-all system. In each district, whoever got the plurality of the vote ended up with all the delegates. This system was ideal for Bentsen because he could concede George Wallace the hard-core 30 percent conservative vote, let the liberal candidates split up their 30 percent, and take everything in the middle. He'd run away with the state's delegate haul, while Wallace and the rest of the contenders went home with nothing. The thinking was that most Democratic candidates would choose not to waste their money on Texas, and would simply let Bentsen collect his ill-gotten jackpot.

Liberals saw this primary-election structure as a demonstration of pure greed by Bentsen. To their way of thinking, Bentsen wanted to nullify their votes because he was unwilling to settle for his proportional share of the delegates. The real kicker of the bill was that it allowed presidential candidates to simultaneously run for another office in the same primary election. Coincidentally, Bentsen faced a senatorial election in 1976 at the same time he was pursuing the presidency. The primary law guaranteed that he wouldn't be forced to choose between the job he wanted (the presidency) and the job he already had (senator).

Bentsen not only shaped the terms of the legislation; he also openly lobbied for it with Democratic legislators. Kent Hance, then a folksy young Democratic state senator from West Texas (and currently the folksy chancellor of Texas Tech University), remembers Bentsen imploring him to support the bill. "He talked to us about it. He talked to me about it. He said he felt that this would get more participation [in the election process], and that he would be the odds-on favorite and would win this primary," says Hance, who later served three terms in the US House before switching parties, at Reagan's urging.

Schieffer, the younger brother of CBS reporter Bob Schieffer (who covered the 1976 presidential race for the network), didn't emerge from this act of political gamesmanship unscathed. Later that year, *Texas Monthly* named him one of the state's ten worst legislators, and in building their case, they made the Bentsen Primary Bill Exhibit A. The magazine branded the law "patently unfair" and bemoaned Schieffer's "garbled mishandling of that affair."[13] (Schieffer eventually became one of the Republican Party's favorite Democrats, joining George W. Bush in an investment group that bought the Texas Rangers baseball team, and serving as ambassador to Australia and Japan during Bush's presidency.) "There was controversy, because it was kind of a lock-in for Bentsen," Hance says. "The Republicans knew that it was a deal for Lloyd Bentsen, and they complained about it, but those complaints didn't go anywhere."

The bill irked liberal Democrats at least as much as it galled Republicans. State representative Ron Waters of Houston expressed the view of many progressives when he said, "We must bury Lloyd Bentsen with his own presidential primary bill."

State senator Babe Schwartz, a wildly colorful orator from the coastal city of Galveston, actually supported Bentsen as a presidential candidate (and later agreed to serve as one of his primary delegates) but had trouble stomaching Schieffer's provision allowing presidential candidates to also run for another office in the same primary election. So Schwartz introduced an amendment that threw out the primary system after the 1976 election cycle. "I was for Lloyd Bentsen, but I didn't want everybody to come along, every time there was an election, and run for more than one position on the same ballot," he recalls. "We were just going to pass it because we all wanted him to be president. But I was more concerned that it might get to be a habit in Texas, where candidates would pick and choose between what they wanted to run for, when they couldn't make up their mind."

When some liberal Democrats initially stonewalled on Schieffer's legislation, Schieffer made no attempt to disguise his motivations. "This sort of thing doesn't help [Bentsen]," he complained, as if that should be the legislature's chief consideration.

State representative Jim Mattox, a liberal Democrat from Dallas, warned that the bill was so obviously written for Bentsen that it was an embarrassment to his candidacy. "The national press is watching us," Mattox said. "You may not want Bentsen to be tried in the national press."

State representative Billie Carr, a legendary liberal warrior from Houston, was so incensed by the primary bill that she threatened to go to Washington and meet with potential presidential candidates who could oppose Bentsen in Texas. (Carr was not one to be trifled with: In her 2002 obituary on the former legislator, Texas political writer Molly Ivins revealed that Carr, a longtime friend and supporter of Bill Clinton, approached him in a White House receiving line shortly after the Monica Lewinsky sex scandal broke and sternly said, "You dumb son of a bitch.")

By the time Schieffer's legislation came along, states were increasingly turning to primaries as a way of choosing delegates for presidential-nomination contests. The turning point came in 1968. That year, Robert Kennedy and Eugene McCarthy battled it out in the Democratic primaries, while Hubert Humphrey used his organizational connections to gobble up delegates without entering a single contest. After the 1968 election, the Democratic National Committee created the McGovern-Fraser Commission, which instituted new reforms aimed at giving grassroots party members more weight in the nomination process and reducing the clout of party bosses. South Dakota senator George McGovern, the commission's cochair, became its first major beneficiary when he used the new rules to carry him to the 1972 Democratic presidential nomination. The Republican Party followed the Democratic example and opened up their nomination system. In 1968, thirteen states held presidential primaries. By 1980, that number had reached thirty-seven.

Bentsen's big-money Texas friendships helped him raise more than a million dollars by early 1975, but over the course of that year it became evident that his campaign had failed to catch fire. It didn't help that his natural constituency—churchgoing Southern moderates—had fallen under the spell of a toothy, little-known Georgia peanut farmer (and former governor) named Jimmy Carter.

Nearly two decades before Bill Clinton brought the term "triangulation" into the modern political lexicon, Carter carefully devised a triangulation strategy to guarantee him the nomination. Early on, he would convince liberals that he was a preferable Southern-fried alternative to that old segregationist warhorse George Wallace. Once he'd knocked Wallace out of contention, he could then persuade Southern conservatives that he was one of them, or at least a more comfortable fit than liberal champions such as Morris Udall or Frank Church.

Because Carter's battle plan required a delicate rhetorical dance with the electorate, he feared Bentsen more than any other candidate going into the '76 race. Bentsen posed a threat because he had the potential to make the same case Carter intended to make. "He had a good start in New Jersey, Virginia, Oklahoma, Tennessee, South Carolina," Carter recalled shortly after securing the '76 Democratic nomination. "But he didn't have his heart in it. He didn't make an all-out nationwide effort, and he faded."[14]

By October 1975, Bentsen decided to scale back his campaign and opt for a regional candidacy in the South and Southwest. Even that modest proposition—which hinged on his hopes for a deadlocked, brokered convention—soon proved unsustainable. Abysmal early showings in the Mississippi and Oklahoma caucuses ensured that Bentsen would be mere ballot filler by the time the New Hampshire primary delivered the official kickoff to primary season. Aware that he stood no chance, but reluctant to call off the dogs in Texas, Bentsen settled for a big push in his home state, where he would run as a favorite-son candidate. By this point, his political limitations, never a hindrance in Texas races, had become obvious to even his home-state backers. "Lloyd was a perfect officeholder, but he was a bland candidate," Schwartz says. "He came off as a quiet, pleasant, personable guy, and the ones that win are the loud, boisterous, good bullshitters."

Bentsen's stubborn determination to thread the ideological needle between conservative and liberal Democrats often meant that he left both factions dissatisfied. Even before he'd made it to the Senate, he irritated liberals in 1970 by making an issue of Yarborough's solidarity with the antiwar movement. A year later, however, he visited Vietnam and returned home an opponent of the war. As a senator, he would adamantly oppose tax increases on crude oil and natural gas at the same moment that he was advocating a new, conservation-incentive tax based on the horsepower of a motor vehicle.

Bentsen's 1976 attempt to run for two offices in the same primary drew harsh attacks from his Democratic challenger in the Senate race, a wonky, combative thirty-three-year-old Texas A&M University economics professor named Phil Gramm. Gramm was a long shot from the beginning, but he had no intention of going down quietly. Although Bentsen was generally viewed as a big-business conservative, Gramm tried to outflank him on the right, even blasting Bentsen for backing an extension of the 1965 Voting Rights Act.

Eight years later, Gramm would win election to the Senate as a Republican, but even as an outmanned underdog in 1976, he displayed all the abrasive cockiness that would later induce a Republican colleague—in a line famously relayed by Molly Ivins—to snort, "Even his friends don't like him."

Although Gramm, and most of his new Republican allies, would use Jimmy Carter as a rhetorical punching bag for much of the 1980s, the 1976 Gramm breathlessly rushed to equate himself with the outsider movement building behind the Democratic front-runner. "There is a new wave of leadership coming to Washington, and I would like to be a part of it," he said during a San Antonio campaign stop on April 29. Gramm couldn't match Bentsen's industry donor list, but he did manage to out-raise Bentsen over the first three months of 1976, bringing in $112,896, including $250 from Colorado beer-industry tycoon Joseph Coors, a conservative Republican.

In January 1976, Gramm filed a complaint with the Federal Election Commission (FEC), accusing Bentsen of diverting federal matching funds, specifically intended for use in his presidential campaign, into his senatorial race. Bentsen vehemently denied the charge, and on April 14, while campaigning in Houston, he displayed a letter from FEC general counsel John Murphy Jr., announcing that the commission had closed its files on Gramm's complaint. "The commission apparently found the charge so lacking in substance that I was not even asked to file an answer," Bentsen gloated, before accusing Gramm of running a deliberately distorted smear campaign against him. Bentsen also insisted that he'd turned down more than $70,000 in federal matching funds since downgrading his presidential campaign to a single-state favorite-son candidacy.[15]

Bentsen spent more than $500,000 to ward off Gramm's pesky primary challenge, but he also kept one hand in the looming presidential contest.[16] At a Saturday, April 10, Democratic gathering in Austin, Bentsen urged the six hundred party members in attendance to support his favorite-son presidential candidacy. Both he and state agriculture commissioner John White, Bentsen's campaign coordinator, insisted that the party's presidential nomination was far from settled, despite Carter's overwhelming national lead. "No candidate is going to walk away with this thing on the first ballot," Bentsen said, proving himself to be less than a stellar prophet. "There will be trading and there will be negotiating. I want to go [to the Democratic National Convention] to fight for Texas and to fight for the things Texans believe in."

All of this sounded suspiciously like a call for the discredited convention tradition of reciprocal back-scratching in smoke-filled rooms, and Carter attempted to persuade Texans that they deserved better. "It's past the time in Texas for people to turn their votes over to a powerful intermediary to cast their vote for them in July in a brokered way," Carter said.[17]

Texas governor Dolph Briscoe, a ranching tycoon from the small South Texas town of Uvalde and a slow-talking, stubbornly cautious politician, initially backed Bentsen in the presidential race. He grew conspicuously cozy with Carter in the weeks leading up to the primary, however, which angered Bentsen loyalists to no end. When Briscoe's turn came to speak at the Austin meeting, he declined to mention Bentsen's favorite-son candidacy.

For the most part, Carter maintained a diplomatic tone toward Bentsen, partly because he knew the Texas senator posed no threat for the nomination, and also because Texas was certain to be a crucial swing state in November. The day before the primary, however, Carter couldn't resist unleashing some of his frustration over what he perceived as blatant inequities in the state's new presidential-primary law. "Texas probably has the most disgraceful primary law in the United States," Carter said during a speech in the mammoth House Chamber of the state capitol. According to the *Houston Chronicle*, Carter said the state's primary system confused voters, and he "inferred that the law was designed to make it difficult for every candidate but Bentsen to get delegate slates on the ballot." With a hint of sardonicism, Carter said the legislature deserved praise for "including a self-destruct clause in the primary bill by which the law will expire at the end of the year."[18]

Carter's Texas delegate slate was a sad-sack collection of people that even his state-headquarters staffers had never heard of, but it didn't seem to make any difference on election day. Although Bentsen comfortably disposed of Gramm in the senatorial race, his awkward, half-hearted attempt to stave off presidential-primary embarrassment in his home state failed. Carter walked away with an overwhelming victory, garnering 48 percent of the popular vote to only 22 percent for Bentsen, and nailing down ninety-two of the state's ninety-eight delegates. Bentsen's horse-trading leverage at the Democratic National Convention amounted to a paltry six delegates.

A year earlier, Bentsen had assumed that the state's open-primary system would lure thousands of Republicans to cross over for him. In fact, the opposite happened. Conservative Democrats, disinterested in their own party's all-but-decided race, connected with Reagan and crossed over into the GOP primary. Bentsen never saw it coming.

During an April 29 San Antonio campaign stop—which found Bentsen and Gramm hustling votes on different floors of the St. Anthony Hotel at the same time—the senator insisted that few real Democrats would cross over and estimated that the Republican primary would draw between 200,000 and 300,000. (The actual number approached 420,000.) A comic low point of sorts for Bentsen's San Antonio visit came during a National Taco Month Breakfast at City Hall when someone ran off with the senator's once-bitten bean taco, much to his evident dismay. If taco theft can be regarded as an omen, it was the first sign that Bentsen was headed for a very bad week. "Bentsen thought that everybody would want to vote in the primary for him," Hance says. "But once he lost the glow of his campaign, and everybody thought the race was decided, that was it."

It is one of the great obscure ironies of modern American politics that a primary meticulously tailored to put a particular Democrat in the White House inadvertently ignited a Republican movement. "The funny thing about it: The whole thing was to help Bentsen, and it didn't help him a lick, it helped Reagan," Hance says. "It's a case of unintended consequences. Many times in politics, you'll set out to go down one road and it completely turns, becomes a different road. And that's what happened, because Bentsen got knocked out early."

Then–lieutenant governor Bill Hobby, a moderate Houston Democrat with a long family political lineage, was a friend of Bentsen's and immediately endorsed his 1976 presidential bid. When Schieffer submitted the presidential-primary legislation, Hobby was quick to give it his blessing. Strangely, however, Hobby—a man whose encyclopedic recall of his days at the state capitol was displayed in his 2010 memoir, *How Things Really Work: Lessons from a Life in Politics*—now says he has absolutely no memory of the Bentsen Primary Bill. He's not alone: While Texas Democrats of the late 1970s bemoaned the bill's damaging impact on their party, it has since become a kind of collective repressed memory. Everyone sees the effect, but few know—or remember—the cause.

The 1975 Bentsen Primary Bill was neither the first nor the last time that Texas lawmakers attempted to bend the election rules for a favorite son seeking national office. In April 1959, with Lyndon Johnson already eyeing the 1960 presidential nomination, the overwhelmingly Democratic legislature created a law that allowed him to be on the state ballot twice in a single election. (He ended up simultaneously running for vice president and for reelection to the Senate, and winning both races.)

In 1979, Hobby pushed hard for a bill that would create a split primary, enabling people to vote in one party's presidential contest while switching parties for down-ballot races. The bill seemed engineered to aid the presidential campaign of former Texas governor John Connally, who had switched from the Democratic Party to the GOP in 1973. The bill would allow Democrats who liked Connally to vote for him in the Republican primary without having to abandon the local and state Democratic races they cared about. Hobby has consistently argued that he had no great regard for Connally and wasn't motivated by a desire to help him. In fact, the bigger concern for Hobby was that conservative Democrats might be attracted to the GOP presidential primary, and he wanted his party to at least be able to hold on to those voters for state and local races. Twelve rebellious senators who became known as the "Killer Bees"—including Babe Schwartz—broke quorum to prevent the bill's passage and hid out a few blocks from the capitol. Hobby eventually gave up on the bill, later calling the entire debacle his biggest mistake in eighteen years as lieutenant governor.

As his Senate career progressed, Bentsen's resistance to ideological dogma put him increasingly out of step with a Democratic Party that had grown more liberal (or, more precisely, less conservative, as Southerners began to abandon the party) in the '70s. Over the course of the Reagan-dominated 1980s, he opposed gun control, supported school prayer, and backed Reagan's crusade to provide aid for the anti-Sandinista rebel forces in Nicaragua. When Democratic presidential nominee Michael Dukakis tabbed Bentsen to be his running mate in 1988, the ideological divide between them was jarring enough for *Time* magazine to dub them "The Odd Couple."

Their ideological incompatibility, however, was soon overshadowed by an October 1988 debate in which Bentsen forever sealed the callow public image of Republican vice presidential nominee Dan Quayle. At one point, Quayle fended off a question about his youth by saying, "I have as much experience in the Congress as Jack Kennedy did when he sought the presidency."

Bentsen's famous response: "I served with Jack Kennedy. I knew Jack Kennedy. Jack Kennedy was a friend of mine. Senator, you're no Jack Kennedy." The cruelty of the jab was only intensified by

Bentsen's oddly courteous delivery. For anyone who viewed the exchange with the sound off, Bentsen's frozen smile might have suggested that he was inviting a colleague over to the house for tea and crumpets.

The Dukakis-Bentsen team failed to win the 1988 general election, but Bentsen came out of the race, much like 1968 Democratic second-banana Edmund Muskie, with his reputation enhanced. Also, in an odd bit of political symmetry, he benefited from the old LBJ election law and was able to win another term in the Senate at the same he lost his race for vice president. In 1993, Bentsen left the Senate to serve as treasury secretary under Bill Clinton, helping to massage the controversial NAFTA treaty through Congress.

By December 1994, when Bentsen retired from public life and returned to Texas, politics in his home state had turned upside down. In fact, no Texas Democrat has won a statewide election since that year. Bentsen's push to create a 1976 presidential primary in Texas was hardly the only cause of this realignment, but it certainly lit the fuse.

CHAPTER 3

THE TWO RAYS

When it came time for the Reagan campaign to pick the leader of their Texas team, their options were slim. Unlike North Carolina, where they could count on Jesse Helms, or New Hampshire, where they had loose-cannon Governor Meldrim Thompson solidly in their corner, in Texas they could scarcely find a Republican county commissioner or district judge willing to sign their name to the cause.

They quickly settled on Ray Barnhart, a brash, cantankerous forty-eight-year-old entrepreneur who worked as an underground-utilities contractor. An Illinois native, Barnhart had studied speech and theater arts at Marietta College in Ohio and taught at his alma mater for four years. In 1955, he concluded that he couldn't support a family on his annual salary of $3,050, so he, his wife Jacqueline, and their two young daughters moved down to Pasadena (later to become the home of the mega-honky-tonk Gilley's, and the setting for the movie *Urban Cowboy*), where he quickly started his own business. "I dug ditches for a living," he says with undisguised pride. "I was putting in water and sewer lines." Over the next several years, Barnhart also developed an interest in politics, serving a short stint as a Pasadena city council member, and riding the GOP coattails of Richard Nixon and John Tower to a seat in the Texas House of Representatives in 1972.

Barnhart looked a bit like former New York Yankees manager Casey Stengel, with a regal beak of a nose, a sharp, jutting jaw, and eyes that were perpetually animated slits, all covered by a thin mop of Grecian Formula gray. Like Stengel, he was also innately hammy, with a personality—surely informed by his theatrical training—that seemed to bask in the glow of the spotlight. "He loved to hear himself talk," groused Polly Sowell, vice chairman of the Texas Republican Party in the mid-'70s and a dedicated Ford supporter. "He was a thorn in everybody's side because he was so loud and outspoken and unwilling to compromise or work with anybody. He was very hard-nosed and very domineering. So he was not the best person for Reagan." Even Barnhart's friends would agree that he often reveled in the sport of political mud-wrestling, although, unlike Sowell, they generally found him more inspiring than exasperating.

Barnhart was one of thirteen Republicans in the Texas House's freshman class of 1973, a group that also included Ray Hutchison, a bright forty-year-old Dallas bond lawyer, and Kay Bailey, a divorced twenty-nine-year-old former Houston TV reporter. Hutchison and Bailey bonded during their first term in the legislature, and Hutchison would ultimately leave his first wife to marry her. As Kay Bailey Hutchison, she would lose a 1982 congressional primary race to Steve Bartlett before going on to serve two decades in Lloyd Bentsen's old US Senate seat.

Hutchison and Bailey were pragmatic legislative deal-makers, but Barnhart was a hard-headed ideologue who'd go to the mat with anyone trying to expand the role of the state government. In 1974, he helped foil a state constitutional convention by vehemently opposing an equal-opportunity education measure because he believed it would result in tuition being eliminated from the state's public universities.

In September of that year, only a month after Gerald Ford became president, Barnhart pushed a resolution through the State Republican Convention expressing "very deep concern" over the direction being taken by the new administration. In particular, Barnhart objected to Ford's offer of amnesty for Vietnam War draft dodgers and his choice of Nelson Rockefeller as vice president. "The compromising atmosphere of Washington is undermining the conservative mandate so loudly proclaimed by Texans and all Americans in the election of 1972," the resolution stated. That November, Barnhart—already perceived as one of the most divisive figures in the legislature—lost his reelection bid to liberal Democrat Bill Caraway, a history teacher at San Jacinto Junior College.

In November 1975, while serving as Harris County Republican Chairman, Barnhart received a call from John Sears, the architect of Reagan's budding presidential campaign. Barnhart had never met Reagan—though he'd admired him from a distance since the '64 speech for Goldwater—and he didn't know Sears from Spiro Agnew. But Sears said he wanted to come down to Houston to talk about the Texas campaign for Reagan. Barnhart agreed but insisted that they include Harris County's precinct chairmen in the discussions, because he figured "they were going to be key to the campaign if Reagan was going to win."

Barnhart called his friend Jimmy Lyon, the chairman and CEO of the River Oaks Bank in Houston, and asked if they could use Lyon's board room for the meeting. After breaking down campaign strategy for more than an hour with Barnhart, Lyon, and forty precinct chairs, Sears announced that he wanted to speak to Barnhart privately. They sat down on a sofa in front of the boardroom fireplace. "He said, 'Put it together. Reagan wants you to head his campaign,'" Barnhart recalls. "I said, 'Oh, gosh, but this campaign is going to have to be different. The Dallasites, they're the elitists, and we here in Houston and the rural parts of Texas are the unwashed. I'll call you and tell you how I'm going to organize it.'"

The Houston-Dallas split had defined and fractured the Texas Republican Party for as long as anyone could remember. Both cities had plenty of oil millionaires and fat-cat bankers and developers, but their sensibilities were unmistakably different. Dallas aspired to sophistication and gentility, while Houston had a new-money earthiness, which its detractors would call vulgarity, and a general intolerance for highfalutin' ostentatiousness.

Politically, the Dallas GOP was pragmatic and middle-of-the-road. Its leaders wanted to hold the line on taxes, but they didn't have any big gripes with the Kennedy-Johnson premise that government could be a positive force for social change in America. Houston was populist and unabashedly conservative. Its leaders saw their personal freedoms under attack from encroaching government regulation and an expanding welfare state, and they were on a crusade to stop it. Dallas had dominated the Republican Party for years, and its country-club, don't-make-waves aesthetic was emblematic of the party's pallid history of failure.

Jeff Bell, who served as the national research director of Citizens for Reagan, joined the Texas campaign in early April, and was immediately struck by the Houston-Dallas GOP fissure. "My first impression was that we had an enormous struggle," Bell recalls. "The feeling was that the Texas Republican Party was an upscale party, a country-club party, and if only they voted, Reagan would lose to Ford. There was a Dallas overtone to the Ford side, as well as a country-club overtone. It was seen as the center of Texas at that time. But Houston was out of it. They were less establishmentarian."

In putting his campaign team together, Barnhart sought denominational as well as geographic balance. West Texas, with its dusty plains and roughneck oil wildcatters, didn't cotton to the country-club set, and given its own remote location, it was even more alienated from the party machinery than the Houston crowd. Ernest Angelo Jr., one of the first Republicans anyone in Midland had known, looked like a perfect cochair. It didn't hurt that Angelo was a Catholic, and Barnhart, who was a Methodist, wanted to broaden the campaign's Christian base.

With that in mind, Barnhart picked Barbara Staff, a GOP activist and supremely devout Baptist, to be the third campaign chair. Staff gave them a connection, if not a particularly powerful one, in the state's second-biggest city, and Barnhart counted on her to bend the ears of her many fellow parishioners at the First Baptist Church in Dallas. W. A. Criswell, the church's pastor, had already established himself as a seminal figure in the rise of social conservatism among Southern evangelicals, a movement that ultimately helped elevate Reagan to the presidency in 1980 and led to the formation of Jerry Falwell's crusading Moral Majority.

Criswell had been among the loudest fear mongers back in 1960 when some Protestant ministers suggested that John Kennedy's Catholicism would spur him to make policy decisions based on directives from the pope. Criswell publicly blasted Roman Catholicism as a "political tyranny" and recommended that all Catholics be barred from public office. Like many other Southern Baptists, he also resisted the social tug of racial integration through most of the 1960s.[19] At Criswell's peak, however, his mega-church attracted a loyal congregation of up to twenty-six thousand, and the pastor's willingness to make political stands from the pulpit made him a valuable ally in conservative circles. "I wanted a Baptist, because there are so many Baptists in Texas," Barnhart recalls about his decision to put Staff in charge of the North Texas effort. "I also wanted a woman, because, frankly, women do all the work in political campaigns. The men are the big deals and talk big, but it's the women who do the work."

When Barnhart really likes someone, the most gushing praise he can think to offer is to call them a "dandy person." It's a term that he throws around frequently when he talks about Angelo and Lyon. Angelo was born in St. Paul, Minnesota, where his father worked as a college professor. The family relocated when the elder Angelo took a job with the Louisiana Department of Agriculture, and Angelo stayed in the Bayou State to study petroleum engineering at LSU. In 1952, as a college freshman, he got his first taste of political controversy, when he wrote a letter to the editor of the school newspaper in defense of controversial Wisconsin senator Joe McCarthy, then the communist-hunting head of the Senate's Permanent Subcommittee on Investigations. "The letter was controversial enough that the editor of the paper, who was a fraternity brother of mine, called me and asked, 'Do you really want to run this letter?' I said, 'Well, yeah.' My English teacher chastised me greatly over it and I thought I was going to flunk the course," Angelo says.

Because Democrats controlled politics in Louisiana, when Angelo began voting, he voted in Democratic primaries. In 1956, he moved to Midland to take a job with Gulf Oil. By 1964, when he started his own oil-and-gas company, Discovery Exploration, politics had developed into his deepest passion. He began devouring conservative magazines such as *National Review* and *Human Events*, and worked with like-minded petroleum-industry colleagues to help Barry Goldwater carry Midland over Texas native son Lyndon Johnson in the 1964 presidential election. "We started a Young Republicans club and had a mimeograph machine in one of the guys' garages," Angelo remembers with a laugh. "We put out a monthly with reproduced articles from different sources and mailed them to about three or four hundred people who were not in the Young Republicans. Then we started trying to find people to run for office."

One of the people they found, a fellow Midland oil man named Frank Kell Cahoon, swam against LBJ's powerful Democrat tide of '64 and won a seat in the Texas House of Representatives. In January 1965, when he took office, Cahoon was the lone Republican in the Texas legislature, up against 149 Democrats in the House and 31 in the Senate.

Necessity and desperation compelled Angelo to make the transition from GOP activist, working for other candidates, to a political candidate himself. In 1968, while he was running for county chairman, the party's inability to find a candidate for the state senatorial race resulted in Angelo filing at the last minute. He lost the election, but pulled in more than 40 percent of the vote and carried Midland.

In 1972, his neighbor and friend Tom Craddick, a state representative who a generation later would become a notoriously divisive Texas Speaker of the House, urged Angelo to run for mayor of Midland, as a way of helping Craddick save his seat. "The Democrats were gearing up to really make it hard on him," Angelo says. "We expected the mayor's office to be potentially used against him, since the person running for it was a former Democratic county chairman. So I got talked into running." Initial election returns showed Angelo losing by 500 votes out of 10,000 cast. Late that night, election workers at one of the precincts realized they'd made a statistical error, and Angelo wound up the victor by 150 votes.

By the time Angelo met Barnhart in 1975, the Midland-Houston axis of hard-core GOP conservatives was firmly established. "We got to be friends pretty quick," Angelo says. "I was trying to find people to get involved with the Reagan campaign and so was he. We were trying to get people who had higher positions in the state than we had, but we couldn't find anybody to get involved. So we finally decided that we might as well do it ourselves."

The combination of Barnhart, Angelo, and Staff didn't exactly stir panic attacks among Ford operatives such as Beryl Milburn, the cotton-haired grand dame of the Texas GOP (and first cousin to conservative intellectual titan William F. Buckley Jr.), who was state director for the Ford campaign. At the Ford team's first press conference in Austin, she spoke for many Ford partisans when a reporter asked her about Reagan's Texas campaign. Milburn responded that she wasn't worried, because there was no one "of substance" involved with it. "That was pretty accurate, really," Angelo concedes. "But it really motivated me and Ray to bust a gut on it, which we did."

With considerable help from John Tower, the Ford campaign had put together a formidable delegate slate in Texas. In addition to Milburn, they had former gubernatorial nominee Paul Eggers, state representative Jim Nowlin from San Antonio, and prominent Republican figures such as Hal DeMoss in Houston and Roger Hunsaker in Fort Worth. The biggest name that Barnhart and Angelo boasted, aside from themselves, was state senator Betty Andujar from Fort Worth, the earnest matriarch of Tarrant County GOP politics.

Barnhart and Angelo complemented each other well, because Barnhart was volcanic—quick to exuberance and equally quick to anger—while Angelo was more reflective and diplomatic. Jeff Bell remembers Barnhart as "a passionate guy who was very sophisticated about the party but was unusually values-driven as a party activist." Barnhart wasn't awed by anyone, and for all his zealous commitment to Reagan himself, he didn't hesitate to tangle with members of the candidate's national campaign staff.

Angelo recalls:

The advance people for the campaign come in ahead of the candidate. They're very authoritarian and they tell you what to do. Well,
Ray didn't operate that way. He ended up in confrontations on a
pretty frequent basis with Reagan advance guys. There was one
really sharp-looking guy who looked like, as Ray put it, a German
storm trooper. Ray finally told this guy he didn't want him to set
foot in Texas again during the campaign. He said, "Don't ever let
me know you're in the state." I never would have done that, but it
probably needed to be done.

Barnhart and Angelo also shared a sense that they didn't fit
in with the Texas GOP establishment. They would go to State
Republican Executive Committee (SREC) meetings and propose
resolutions that had no chance of passing just to test the SREC's
conservative will. At state conventions, they would hand-pick candidates to run against committee members they viewed as insufficiently right-wing. Their plan was to gradually build a conservative
majority of the state committee.

The distinctions between "true conservatives" such as
Barnhart and Angelo, and the "country-club moderates" who ran
the party seemed profound to the players involved. In truth, they
had much more to do with style than substance. The country-
club set, like the hard-core conservative crowd, wanted low tax
rates and a business climate in which companies could operate
unfettered by government regulation. They similarly griped about
what they perceived to be abuses in the welfare system, and considered a balanced federal budget to be a high priority. They
wanted the United States to maintain a strong national defense
and maintain a tough stance with the Soviet Union, although
they also welcomed the thaw in relations between the two super-

powers, engineered by Henry Kissinger, secretary of state under both Nixon and Ford.

The conservatives simply cared more deeply about all these things. They not only viewed Lyndon Johnson's Great Society programs as expensive and inefficient, they objected to them on moral grounds: In the minds of Barnhart and Angelo, the Great Society— and much of Franklin Roosevelt's New Deal thirty years earlier— had sapped the initiative, the self-sufficiency, the lift-yourself-up-by-your-bootstraps toughness that they considered integral to the American spirit. They saw high income taxes as more than an inconvenience or an impediment to investment: They saw them as overweening government trampling on the rights of the individual.

They brought a comparable fervor to social issues: opposing the landmark 1973 *Roe v. Wade* Supreme Court decision, which legalized abortion in the United States; supporting the concept of daily prayer in public schools; and vehemently opposing enforced school busing. They viewed all negotiations with the Soviet Union as suspicious and fretted that Ford and Kissinger were selling out American strategic interests.

Ultimately, the chasm between the two GOP factions often boiled down to personality differences, style points, and how intensely they held to their beliefs. As Ray Hutchison says, "It was almost about the language and the attitudes." While Barnhart epitomized the scrappy Houston wing of the Texas GOP, Hutchison became the face of the more genteel Dallas wing. Burly and bespectacled, he alternately dazzled and perplexed his fellow legislators with his heavy reliance on fancy five-dollar words. In a state with an extremely limited Republican talent pool, Hutchison quickly rose to the top of his class, with his name tossed around as a potential gubernatorial candidate not long after joining the Texas House in 1973. *Texas Monthly* consistently praised him for his command of policy and his legislative skills, stating that Hutchison "has, and

displays more, innate intelligence than anyone else [in the House]."
The same qualities that impressed so many with Hutchison—his
eloquence and his sense of decorum—struck his detractors, particularly within the party's extreme right wing, as snobbery and
phoniness.

All of this came to a head during the Ford-Reagan primary clash.
Hutchison had become state party chairman in 1975, and he was
careful to maintain a public neutrality on the presidential race. It
quickly became obvious to both sides, however, that Hutchison
favored Ford. Sowell said,

> I think Ray was supporting Ford. And one of the considerations was
> both Ray and I were up for reelection ourselves that September,
> so we had to be fairly careful about what we said and did. Many of
> the people voting for Reagan in the primary were not people who
> were active in the Republican Party. They were not people who
> went to precinct conventions or state conventions, or would have
> worked for or against Ray and me when we were running for office.
> So it was a very unusual situation and difficult for politicians.

(Sowell attracted national attention in 2006 after Vice President
Dick Cheney accidentally shot his friend Harry Whittington during
a hunting excursion at the Armstrong Ranch. Sowell had been a
frequent guest of the ranch's owners, Anne and Tobin Armstrong,
and was interviewed by CNN about it.)

Staff, who ran in the same Dallas GOP circles with Hutchison,
says she has "bitter" memories of Hutchison from the '76 campaign. "We would often cross paths at different candidate forums,
and he was unbearable," she says. "He was just a snob and he
translated our campaign as disloyalty to the party. So, of course,
I hated his guts."

Staff says her Dallas County GOP women's group also developed a more personal distaste for Hutchison after he left his first

wife, Mary, and married Kay Bailey. "Mary was a housewife who belonged to a Republican Women's Club in the White Rock Lake area. Everybody loved her," Staff says. "She was just a sweet lady who was raising her children. So when the marriage broke up, most of the Republican women took sides with Mary. Unfortunately, she began to drink a lot after the divorce."

Hutchison was so sensitive to charges that he worked behind the scenes to help Ford in '76, he fired off a short letter to *Texas Monthly* during his 1978 campaign for governor, denying the magazine's assertion that he had opposed Reagan in the '76 presidential primary: "Never did I take a position of support for either Mr. Reagan or Mr. Ford during the 1976 Presidential Primary election in Texas. I maintained that as party chairman I had a responsibility to remain neutral. Obviously I could not meet that responsibility were I to take a position for or against any candidate opposed in the primary."[20] If Hutchison himself did not explicitly back Ford, most of the party leaders did, including his future wife Kay Bailey, whom Ford had appointed earlier that year as vice chairwoman of the National Transportation Safety Board.

These days, Hutchison continues to emphasize that he was "very, very close to both sides" and considered himself a friend to both Ford and Reagan, but his avowed neutrality never convinced the Reagan diehards, who tended to put all Republicans in either a "friend" or "enemy" box. Going into the 1976 primary, Hutchison was widely seen as the Texas GOP's brightest light, but only two years later he would suffer one of the most humbling, humiliating electoral defeats in the state's history.

CHAPTER 4

LYON'S GAMBIT

Ronald Reagan needed money. Desperately. Going into the March 23 North Carolina primary, Reagan's presidential campaign was nearly $2 million in debt, and most of its staffers were working without pay. Despite his best efforts, campaign manager John Sears couldn't find any banks willing to provide new loans to Reagan's cash-strapped organization.

Sears deserved at least some of the blame for the crisis. Widely admired in GOP circles for his tactical brilliance and media savvy, Sears was not particularly disciplined when it came to allocating campaign resources. In addition, the Reagan campaign was suffering ill effects from the US Supreme Court's January 30, 1976, *Buckley v. Valeo* decision, which overturned part of the 1974 Federal Election Campaign Act. That law had created the Federal Election Commission and set up a new system for financing presidential primaries and general elections. Under the new law, presidential candidates were eligible for federal funding that matched the amount of private money that campaign had brought in, assuming the candidate raised more than $5,000 in each of at least twenty states.

Among its other effects, the *Buckley* decision invalidated the FEC, because the Court determined that the commission was an executive body, and Congress, by granting itself the power to select four of the FEC's six members, had taken some authority that

rightfully belonged to the president. In the wake of the Court decision, Congress worked to create a new structure for the FEC, but
in the meantime, with no commission around to disperse matching
funds, presidential candidates had to patiently wait for their federal money. By late March, the Reagan campaign was owed more
than $1 million in federal funds, with no idea when—or if—it would
receive the money.

On the day of the North Carolina primary, Sears went to Reagan
with a proposition. Given the campaign's bleak financial state, Sears
suggested that the candidate abandon his efforts in Wisconsin and
fly back to Los Angeles to tape a thirty-minute, nationally televised
fundraising commercial. Reagan, who had been trying for weeks
to convince skeptical campaign staffers that he had the ability to
raise considerable money on TV, instantly agreed. There was only
one question: How were they going to pay for the TV appearance?

In utter desperation, they called on Jimmy Lyon, an ardent
Reagan supporter who ran the largest independent bank in
Houston. Barnhart had held his first meeting with Sears at Lyon's
bank, and subsequently drafted Lyon to serve as the Texas finance
chairman for Citizens for Reagan. Houston was a city driven, in
large part, by the energy of entrepreneurial transplants from other
parts of the country, but the forty-eight-year-old Lyon was a native
and a Houstonian to the core. He'd gone to San Jacinto High School
and stayed in town to attend Rice University and the University of
Houston. After serving in the Marines during World War II, he came
back to Houston, voraciously gobbled up real estate properties,
developed new Houston subdivisions, and built the popular ocean-
front USS Flagship Hotel in Galveston on the historic Pleasure Pier.
In 1962, he bought controlling interest of River Oaks Bank, and
over the twenty-eight years that he served as its chairman, the
bank never reported an unprofitable year.

A tightly wound worrywart, Lyon was a devout Baptist and an unyielding social conservative. In 1985, he loaned $121,000 to a group opposing a Houston referendum that would ban discrimination against gays and lesbians employed by the city. During that same period, he began a lengthy romantic relationship with Anita Bryant, the former singer, beauty queen, and Florida orange-juice pitch-woman who'd essentially sabotaged her own career in the late '70s by becoming the nation's most vociferous crusader against gay rights. In 1990, Lyon married one of Bryant's best friends, a Georgian named Desiree Dobson. "Jimmy was a Bible-believing Christian, and he was very intense," remembers Bell, who spent much of April 1976 working out of the Reagan headquarters in Houston. "He always seemed to be in an emotional state about the way the campaign was going. There were always horrible things that were going wrong, things that we weren't doing that we should have been doing. Personally, he was always in a state of crisis."

Despite Lyon's bouts of anxiety, Barnhart deeply valued his presence in the campaign, at least partly because Lyon was the only Texas banker he knew in the mid-'70s who was willing to declare himself a Republican. Although he'd been active in the party for years—even earning the Harris County GOP's "Mr. Republican" title in 1969—Lyon had never thrown himself as fully into political battle as he did with Reagan in 1976.

In March 1976, Barnhart received a call from an obviously agitated Lyon.

> Jimmy said, "I've got a problem. Can you come over?" So I drove over to his bank and Jimmy said, "Well, the [Reagan] campaign's broke. They want me to loan them $100,000. And I don't know what to do. I've got stockholders here in the bank to answer to." I said, "Jimmy, there is no question of what you have to do. If you truly believe in Reagan and in our cause, you've got no choice. You've

got to loan it to the campaign. You do it like they do in the movies. They finance movies and then they get paid."

While Lyon pondered his options, there was internal debate in the upper echelons of Reagan's national campaign over whether the loan would violate any election laws. Finally, Loren Smith, chief counsel for the campaign, concluded that the loan was legal. Barnhart's pep talk had swayed Lyon, but he still needed one extra dose of assurance. He called Bruce Eberle, Reagan's direct-mail guru, to get a sense of whether the campaign would be able to raise enough money to reimburse him. Eberle convinced him that the campaign would pay him back, and Lyon sent his payment.[21]

Reagan spent days polishing the fundraising speech and five hours taping it at a Hollywood commercial studio. NBC, the only major network to show an interest in it, gladly preempted its sitcom bomb *The Dumplings* to air the speech on Wednesday, March 31. Starting slowly, Reagan questioned Ford's assertions that the economy was rebounding from the 1975 recession and insisted that the president's proposal for $28 billion in tax cuts and spending reductions hadn't gone far enough. He also took issue, in blunt terms, with those who argued that there were no significant philosophical differences between himself and Ford, and he attempted to turn one of Ford's perceived assets—his superior governmental experience—into a liability.

Before Richard Nixon appointed him vice president, Mr. Ford was a congressman for twenty-five years. His concern, of necessity, was the welfare of his congressional district. For most of his adult life he has been a part of the Washington establishment. Most of my adult life has been spent outside of government. Now, Mr. Ford places his faith in the Washington establishment. This has been evident in his appointment of former congressmen and longtime government workers to positions in his administration. Well,

I don't believe that those who have been part of the problem are necessarily the best qualified to solve those problems.

These critiques were fairly civil, however, compared to what was coming: an all-out assault on Ford and Kissinger's foreign policy that accused them of diminishing America's standing in the world and leaving it at grave risk of attack from the Soviet Union. In Asia, the Middle East, Latin America, and Africa, Reagan asserted, the United States was "wandering without aim." As he did from time to time on the campaign trail, Reagan, near the end of his speech, overstepped the facts by using dubious source material. He said Kissinger believed the United States must accept a position of subservience to the Soviet Union, and added that the secretary of state had essentially written off any possibility that the Soviet Union's Eastern European satellites could be liberated. "Dr. Kissinger is quoted as saying that he thinks of the United States as Athens and the Soviet Union as Sparta: 'The day of the US is past and today is the day of the Soviet Union.' And he added, 'My job as secretary of state is to negotiate the most acceptable second-best position available.'"

The Kissinger quote was taken from a not-yet-published book by Retired Admiral Elmo Zumwalt Jr., who claimed that Kissinger made the statement to him on a 1970 train ride to the Army-Navy football game in Philadelphia. Not surprisingly, Kissinger bitterly denied that he'd ever said any such thing, and the palpable enmity between Reagan and Kissinger would only deepen in the weeks leading up to the Texas primary. The unusual specter of the nation's secretary of state interjecting himself in a primary campaign did Ford no favors, because by 1976 Kissinger had become red meat for the GOP's extreme conservative wing.

Regardless of its factual merits, Reagan's televised speech was a resounding success. It drew 13 million viewers and ultimately brought in more than $1.5 million in campaign contributions. At least temporarily, the campaign's financial crisis had lifted. Johnny Carson, the most prominent employee of the network that aired it, had this to say about Reagan's TV performance: "It would be funny if he turned out to be NBC's only hit."[22] Barnhart remembers: "They cut that commercial and for days after that, they opened up tons of mail. It was the most successful fundraising thing that had ever been done."

Lyon's loan not only kept Reagan's campaign afloat, it signaled, a full month before the Texas primary, how critical Reagan's Texas team was to his presidential prospects. Even among Reagan loyalists, however, Lyon's brand of Christian conservatism could sometimes seem narrow-minded. This became an issue when Lyon couldn't disguise his discomfort around Arthur Finkelstein, a thirty-year-old media consultant that the Reagan campaign had sent to Houston to help out with the Texas-primary effort. Not only was Finkelstein Jewish, which made him something of a novelty for Lyon, he was also a closeted homosexual, which almost certainly would have appalled Lyon if he'd known about it. (Finkelstein didn't come out of the closet until 2005, when he announced that he'd married his male partner in a civil ceremony in Massachusetts.)

"Jimmy was a real character," Bell says. "We would have strategy meetings, and Arthur and Jimmy would be there. At one point, Arthur was laughing in a way, because it was just so naive and innocent, but he'd say to Jimmy: 'You really don't like Jews, do you? You don't really approve of me.' He was actually laughing about it. It wasn't a shouting match, like it might sound."

Accustomed to controlling every detail of his business environment, Lyon often found the organized chaos of a presidential campaign too nerve-racking to handle. "Jimmy loved to talk, and when he called, it would take thirty or forty minutes every time, just hashing and rehashing everything," Angelo says. "He didn't have the hands-on political feel that Ray and I had. So he was panicked that we weren't going to win. On the day of the [Texas] primary, he actually was throwing up most of the afternoon, he was so nervous about it."

In 1981, Reagan rewarded Lyon for his role as the sugar daddy of the Texas campaign by appointing him to the board of directors of the Federal National Mortgage Association, also known as Fannie Mae. That same year, he again came through when his political hero needed money. Nancy Reagan had decided that she wanted to redecorate the White House, and opted to pay for it with private funds. Holmes Tuttle, one of Reagan's California confidantes, asked Lyon to cohost a Houston fundraising party for the redecoration project. The party drew twelve wealthy Houstonians; they donated $60,000 to the cause, while Lyon himself cut a check for $10,000. Lyon's steadfast conservative values would even lead him to support former Nevada senator Paul Laxalt—national chairman of Reagan's '76 campaign—in the 1988 presidential race over Texas favorite son George Bush. Laxalt was the longest of long shots in the 1988 race, but he appealed to Lyon because he had iron-clad conservative credentials and, most importantly, he was one of Reagan's closest friends.

Lyon's crucial role in Reagan's 1976 campaign has been undersold over the years, with only Craig Shirley giving it much attention. In his 1990 autobiography, *Ronald Reagan: An American Life*, Reagan wrote, "[We] gambled much of our remaining campaign funds" to buy airtime for the thirty-minute speech. In truth, they gambled with Jimmy Lyon's funds, not their own. But it was a gamble that paid big dividends for both Lyon and the campaign.

CHAPTER 5

THE TRUTH SQUAD

Ronald Reagan's afternoon arrival in Dallas on Monday, April 5, 1976, officially launched the Texas presidential primary campaign, but it was only the second biggest story in the state that day. That morning, native Texan and legendary mogul Howard Hughes died en route from Acapulco to a Houston hospital. Over the next several weeks, breathless accounts of the eccentric recluse's physical deterioration and conflicting stories about his will dominated Texas media coverage, at times even overshadowing the battle between Ford and Reagan.

By the time he landed in Texas, Reagan had found his message. His success in North Carolina and the overwhelmingly positive response to his thirty-minute televised speech convinced Reagan not only to amp up the aggressive attacks on Ford but also make foreign policy and America's military strength the focus of his campaign. Practically the first words out of Reagan's mouth when he addressed reporters at Dallas's Hilton Inn concerned what he called the nation's "declining military status," and he added that the United States had "frittered away a clear military superiority" over the previous decade.

Reagan's new line of diatribe was fueled as much by practicality as ideological passion. Over the first three months of 1976, he'd simply failed to gain much traction with his pet domestic themes:

government waste and overweening federal control over individual rights. For one thing, it wasn't easy to tag Ford as a tax-and-spend liberal. The most notable part of his domestic record, after all, had been his thirty-seven vetoes in the span of a year and a half, most of them overt rejections of Democratic spending initiatives. As a result, Reagan had devoted much of his energy in the early primaries to critiques of the Democratic Congress—a popular line of attack among the GOP faithful, to be sure, but not one that would persuade wavering voters to toss aside an incumbent Republican president.

In Texas, Reagan would find the perfect audience for his new sermon. The state not only had a high concentration of military bases, particularly in San Antonio, but also had a culture that ate up the kind of tough talk Reagan had begun dishing out. Reagan's trip to Dallas gave him a jump on Ford, who wouldn't make his first campaign stop in Texas until four days later. But, in a sense, Reagan had been stumping for votes in the state ever since he left the California governor's mansion in January 1975.

Between January and November—when he formally entered the race—Reagan made seven stops in Texas. He spoke to the Texas Manufacturing Association in Dallas, to sales and marketing executives in Houston, to former Vietnam War POWs in San Antonio, and to the state GOP in Beaumont. He brought down the house at Houston's St. Joseph Building Fund Dinner, charmed the San Antonio Chamber of Commerce, and touted the glories of entrepreneurship when the National Soft Drink Association met in Dallas.

All this face time in the Lone Star State might explain why many Texas conservatives looked to him, well before he'd made his plans known, with an intensity that bordered on desperation. In the summer and early fall of 1975, Reagan was flooded with letters from Texas supporters who saw him as the last, best chance for saving the republic. The frustration and anger in some of these letters could easily be mistaken for missives from Tea Party activists thirty-five years later. In some cases, a post-Watergate disgust with all things Republican prompted calls for Reagan to break his ties to the party and run as an independent, possibly with George Wallace. Jan Norris of Houston, in a June 18, 1975, letter, captured the feeling of impatience among many Reagan loyalists: "Ronald, you're going to have to get off your duff . . . make a move . . . charge! Let's win one for the Gipper."

Reagan, in what would become his standard reply to such exhortations, responded: "Your kind words really warmed my heart. At the present time, however, I am not prepared to announce my decision about the presidency, although I will do so before the first of the year. In the interval, much depends on the amount of support that evidences itself, not from the professional politicians, but from the people."

In a letter dated June 20, 1975, Lubbock resident Hiram Parks implored Reagan to abandon the GOP and run as a "Restoration Party" candidate: "We desperately want you to do this, because desperately, this country needs you to be president. . . . The salvation or restoration of the country can no longer depend on the present two parties."

Rosalind Haley of Lubbock, in a letter dated July 17, 1975, that was dripping with admiration/paranoia, demanded a guarantee from Reagan that he wouldn't run for president "in order to bring people into the fold and then turn them over to John Connally."[23]

Some Texans simply worried about the depth of Reagan's commitment to conservative principles. They wanted to make sure that Reagan was opposed to gun control, legalized abortion, and the latest congressional pay raise; that he wouldn't retain Henry Kissinger as secretary of state; and that his recent military briefing from former defense secretary James Schlesinger (under Nixon and Ford) didn't mean that Reagan would be taking policy advice from him. In each case, Sears, Laxalt, or Nofziger responded with polite assurances that Reagan was squarely in the conservative column.

On the first night of his Texas campaign swing, Reagan spoke to an enthusiastic crowd at Bronco Bowl, a popular Dallas arcade/ entertainment venue. The next day, more than two thousand people filled McFarlin Auditorium at Southern Methodist University (SMU) to hear Reagan's Law Day speech. Reagan relentlessly hammered Kissinger, saying the secretary of state was overseeing a weak, inconsistent foreign policy. In particular, he blamed Kissinger for dithering on the issue of Angola. In 1975, the newly liberated African nation had emerged as the latest front in the Cold War, with both the Soviet Union and the United States using proxies and covert aid to influence the outcome of what would become a prolonged civil war. "The United States should have been able to pick up the hotline to the Soviet Union and say, 'You are risking confrontation with us,'" Reagan said. He added that Kissinger had saved his critical words for when he was "packing to go to Moscow" to negotiate a Strategic Arms Limitation Treaty. "Kissinger should have unpacked his bags and said, 'I'll be in Moscow when you observe détente in Angola.'"

Turning to the subject of crime, Reagan—never a fan of the Supreme Court's 1966 *Miranda* ruling, which required police officers to inform suspects of their rights before interrogating them— blasted criminal courts for making decisions based on "technicalities" rather than innocence or guilt. After Reagan asserted his support for the death penalty and opposition to parole for alleged criminals who carried firearms, one SMU student took aim at this tough-on-crime stance. "We ought to lock out people like you and Mr. Nixon," the student said. The overwhelmingly pro-Reagan crowd hissed.[24]

In Reagan's attempt to articulate a common right-wing sentiment—

the country that patriotic Americans had once known was slipping away from them—he could go to startling rhetorical extremes. He not only denounced the use of forced busing to integrate schools, a position shared by most Republicans and many Democrats, but went so far as to advocate a constitutional amendment to ban busing, "if that's the only way to eliminate it." At a late April stop in Waco, he would even defend the minority white government that controlled the predominantly black South African nation of Rhodesia. Reagan said Ford was "running the risk" of violence there with his "unrelenting opposition to the Rhodesian government."

By this stage of the campaign, Reagan had found a way to take the same small-government message he'd been preaching since the '64 Goldwater speech and meld it with an underlying suggestion that the country's moral fiber was crumbling, and that individual initiative, which he regarded as a hallmark of the America he'd grown up in, was under attack. It was a message that particularly resonated with Southern evangelicals, and it enabled Reagan to take supply-side economics from the elitist, intellectual realm of a William F. Buckley Jr. to the populist realm of white Southern churches.

For all of Reagan's obvious appeal to Christian conservatives, however, Barnhart was struck by the candidate's reluctance to overtly trade on religion. He recalls a particular exchange on that subject during the 1976 campaign.

> I picked Reagan and Nancy up at Hobby Airport [in Houston] and we were driving down the Gulf Freeway. I said, "Hey, I've got a change of plans for Saturday night." I told him that when Jimmy Carter came to Texas, he went up to Dallas and spoke at Criswell's huge Baptist church, and he got all kinds of press because he participated in the Sunday morning service. I said, "I've made arrangements for you to participate in that service. It's just going

to get you tons of publicity all over this state." He was silent for a while. Finally, he said, "We're not going to do it." I said, "Not going to do it? We've got 4 million Baptists in this state and they vote like a bloc!" He said, "You don't understand, Ray. My relationship with my God is *my* relationship, and we're not going to abuse it." It floored me.

If Reagan hesitated to broadcast the particulars of his personal faith, he had no such reservations about bringing religious-based social issues to the fore in a way that national Republican leaders generally avoided. Take the example of a Beaumont breakfast speech in April 1976, when Reagan pivoted on the question of education funding until he found the evangelical cause at the core. Making his patented case for state and local control, Reagan called for the federal government to get out of the way of public education. Such a move, Reagan said, might enable the nation to "get God back in the classroom." The room erupted with applause.

Barnhart had set up Reagan's state headquarters in a Houston strip mall at the bustling intersection of Westheimer and Kirby in the middle of an upscale commercial district. It was a cramped, tiny office in a two-story building down the hall from the Harris County Republican Headquarters, and it served its purpose for a few months. As the primary campaign heated up, however, Barnhart moved them three miles southwest, to a much roomier space on Richmond Avenue.

Jeff Bell remembers walking to the headquarters every day from his nearby hotel, asking himself every step of the way how any place on the planet could be so witheringly hot in early spring. In a sense, Texas was Bell's special purgatory, a penance the New Jerseyan had been forced to serve after landing in the Reagan campaign doghouse. It was Bell who had written Reagan's politically disastrous 1975 speech that had called for cutting $90 billion from the federal budget by heaping a bigger burden on the states. The resulting blowback had swiftly pushed him from the category of thirty-one-year-old policy wunderkind to possible campaign liability. "Reagan had gotten attacked for the $90 billion plan, and probably a lot of people—since he lost in New Hampshire so narrowly—blamed it on me," Bell says. "I was more marginalized on the issues. I was the director of research in the campaign, but I was never out with the candidate, and I wasn't involved in as many key speeches as I had been before."

Bell had initially connected with Reagan late in Reagan's gubernatorial tenure, when Bell worked for the Republican Party of California. Bell then took a job in Los Angeles with the law firm of Deaver & Hannaford, where he again found himself in regular contact with Reagan. Mike Deaver and Pete Hannaford were among Reagan's closest friends and confidantes, and Reagan adopted their Wilshire Boulevard office as his base as soon as he left the governor's office. Bell had previously worked at the American Conservative Union with Ron Dear, the Texas Delegates for Reagan chairman. When Bell found himself in hot water with the Reagan campaign, Dear asked John Sears if Bell could be sent down to help in Texas, and Sears agreed. Bell was put in charge of work on the crossover vote. Because Texas didn't have party registration, Democrats were free to vote in the GOP primary, and Bell actively recruited them.

Seeking out conservatives, regardless of party affiliation, he obtained mailing lists with names of Texans who opposed legalized abortion. Along the way, he and Arthur Finkelstein tracked down a North Texas Democrat named Rollie Millirons, who served as the Fort Worth campaign manager for George Wallace. Although Wallace had been a spoiler in the 1968 general election—taking five Southern states as an independent candidate—and a surprising force in the 1972 Democratic race, he'd been paralyzed from the waist down since May 15, 1972, when an assailant named Arthur Bremer shot him at a Laurel, Maryland, shopping center. In 1976, Wallace was both a physical and political shell of his former self, no longer the automatic choice of disaffected white Southerners and no longer formidable enough to strike fear into the hearts of Northern liberals. By the time the campaign reached Texas, everyone but Wallace seemed to recognize that he'd become irrelevant.

When Millirons determined that Wallace had no chance of winning the '76 Democratic nomination, he quickly defected over to the Reagan camp. Finkelstein wanted to put a conservative Democrat on Reagan radio and TV ads around the state, and both he and Bell agreed that Millirons was the ideal choice. "I think we interviewed a few guys and basically agreed that Rollie was our guy because he was fairly presentable and he came across as blue-collar and down-home. He was kind of typecast," Bell remembers. "So we just gave him a script saying that he was a Democrat for George Wallace, but that Wallace was not going to win that year, so people should cross over. We wanted to give a reason for somebody who was oriented to Wallace to not vote for him, to vote for Reagan instead."

This is what Millirons told his fellow Texans: "I've been a Democrat all my life. A conservative Democrat. As much as I hate to admit it, George Wallace can't be nominated. Ronald Reagan can. He's right on the issues. So, for the first time in my life, I'm gonna vote in the Republican primary. I'm gonna vote for Ronald Reagan."

Wallace, who found himself struggling to get the attention of Texas voters, knew that Reagan was plundering his base, so he directly challenged Millirons's premise. At an April 15 campaign rally in El Paso, Wallace belittled Reagan's potential crossover appeal by insisting that he had a better chance of securing the Democratic nomination than Reagan had of knocking off Ford.

Bell also found himself working on another radio ad, featuring someone with considerably more star power than Millirons: John

Wayne. An old Hollywood friend of Reagan's, who had helped the Gipper out as far back as the 1966 gubernatorial race against Pat Brown, Wayne apparently held a grudge against Stuart Spencer, Ford's chief campaign strategist. A centrist California Republican, Spencer had shown himself over the years to be at least as mercenary—and immune to ideology—as Sears. In 1964, he backed Nelson Rockefeller for president over conservative favorite Barry Goldwater, then turned around and ran Reagan's two gubernatorial campaigns, and was now trying to help Ford beat Reagan. To Reagan campaign loyalists, he was like the coach that leaves you for another team and knows how to exploit your weaknesses when he goes up against you.

"John Wayne expressed an interest in doing a radio commercial for Reagan," Bell says. "Wayne was in his last years at that point, and we sent a guy out to California to record the spot. We'd sent a script, but Wayne threw it away and did his own thing, which was mainly an attack on Stuart Spencer. I mean, you don't tell John Wayne, 'No, I'm sorry, Duke, you have to read our script, not do your own.' So we took it and we ran it, even though a lot of it was about Spencer and dated back to clashes they'd had in the gubernatorial races in California."

Another regular at the Houston campaign office was Steve Munisteri, a gawky, black-haired, eighteen-year-old high school senior with a soft, high voice from the small Houston suburb of Hedwig Village. If it's apt to call someone a political prodigy, Munisteri certainly qualified. In 1972, at the age of fourteen, when many of his peers undoubtedly were spending their after-school time playing pickup basketball or trying to meet girls, Munisteri worked phone banks for Richard Nixon and John Tower, and walked door-to-door on behalf of Republican gubernatorial nominee Hank Grover.

Since the age of ten, he'd been particularly taken with Reagan. In 1968, he sat glued to his TV set and watched Reagan deliver a speech from an airport tarmac after arriving at the Republican National Convention. In 1975, with Reagan showing signs of interest in a presidential campaign, Munisteri began collecting any bit of material he could find on the former California governor. In addition to reading countless newspaper and magazine articles, Munisteri located a conservative organization that allowed him to check out 16mm films of Reagan speeches, which he would diligently watch and return. "I just got very fired up about Reagan," Munisteri says. "Ford was a nice man, but dull. I felt like we needed a dramatic shift in direction for the country and he didn't seem to be the type that would lead the charge for that."

Munisteri's unusual prepubescent fascination with GOP politics was spurred by the example of his mother, Theresa, a political activist who had served as the secretary of a Young Republicans club in New Haven, Connecticut, in 1948. "My mom likes to joke that she's the only person alive who worked for all three Bushes, because she was a volunteer for [Senator] Prescott Bush," Munisteri says. Taking a similar path, Munisteri formed a conservative club at Hedwig Village's Memorial High School, attracting twenty members, three of whom became delegates or alternates to the Republican State Convention.

Working afternoons as a volunteer at the Reagan headquarters, Munisteri didn't kid himself about the campaign's bleak prospects going into the Texas primary. "Around the headquarters, people were saying unless [Reagan] had some sort of dramatic win—and even then it might not be enough—he would have to drop out after Texas," Munisteri says. "We wanted him to have a good showing, to go out on a good note."

Conservative activism seemed to dominate every aspect of

Munisteri's life. That summer he would join other young Reaganites on a bus trip from Texas to Kansas City for the Republican National Convention. On that trip, he met his future wife, Deanna Armstrong, then the president of the University of Texas Young Republicans. After their marriage ended in divorce, Munisteri started a long-term relationship with a woman he had met years earlier through the University of Texas chapter of the Young Conservatives of Texas.

Another important GOP contact Munisteri made during this period was Mark Elam, a University of Texas freshman who volunteered in Austin for the 1976 Reagan campaign. Munisteri and Elam helped to create the Texas Forum, the state's first Republican newspaper specifically geared to college students, and they were also founding members of the Young Conservatives of Texas.

As a Reagan volunteer in the state's one undeniably liberal city and a college student on a predominantly liberal campus, Elam found himself in a curious position. "There was an active group of conservatives there, but certainly we were in the minority," Elam says. "This was right at the tail end of the Vietnam War, so it was a different scene on campus at UT then. It was a more radical liberal environment than I think it's been in the years after that point."

Elam's dominant memory of the period is what a polarizing figure Reagan was: commonly ridiculed on the left as a narrow-minded nincompoop and regarded by many traditional Republicans as a man who was damaging their party's reputation with his emphasis on social issues. "There was a big divide, and a lot of it had to do with the issue of abortion and religion in general," Elam says. "I campaigned for Reagan not only in Austin but in my hometown of Conroe, and you could see it there too. Generally, the people who were helping Reagan were conservative religious types, they really weren't classic Republicans."

Elam was in the crowd when Reagan faced the most combative

audience he would see during his Texas campaign, at the Lyndon Johnson Presidential Library near the University of Texas campus. Unlike his appearance at SMU, where he faced a lone college dissident who was easily drowned out by pro-Reagan partisans, Reagan's Austin speech inspired a small but organized protest effort. Picketers marched outside the LBJ Library carrying signs that said, "No Raygun!" Inside, Reagan encountered sporadic heckling. Much of the crowd hooted when he declared his opposition to the legalization of marijuana. When he launched into his trademark Cold War red-meat speech, saying that communist interference, not the actions of the United States, was the cause of internal strife in Chile, Angola, and elsewhere, an angry student stood up and yelled, "Fascist!"

Reagan, who already had a decade of practice verbally sparring with college antiwar protesters in California, had a retort at the ready, albeit one that amounted to the same kind of sweeping generalization that he was complaining about: "I've always wondered about this liberal philosophy that says, 'How dare you call someone a communist, you fascist!'" Pro-Reagan students, including Elam, cheered wildly.

Dating back to his 1964 speech for Goldwater, Reagan had always been stirred to his greatest heights of righteous indignation when he settled on the topic of national security. The Reagan best remembered now by his admirers—affable, avuncular, sunny, and optimistic—had little in common with the stern Cold Warrior on the stump in Texas in April 1976, warning that America was slipping fast and headed for grave danger. Occasionally, he would employ a lighter touch. In Longview, where an eight-minute motel meeting with city leaders netted him a handy $23,000 in campaign funds, he decried high taxes by saying, "You wonder why they call it take-home pay. That's because it's too little to go home by itself."

But domestic matters had become minor diversions from the real substance of his campaign. By the time he arrived in Texas, Reagan had found a single issue that encapsulated his message that Ford was spineless, easily manipulated, and not respected around the world: the Panama Canal. In a way, it was an unlikely source of campaign alchemy. The man-made waterway connecting the Atlantic and Pacific Oceans had been a fact of life for so long that few Americans gave it any thought. Those who'd bothered to study the history of the canal knew that President Theodore Roosevelt backed Panamanian independence from Colombia primarily so he could have leverage to negotiate an advantageous canal treaty for the United States.

The treaty had been a source of resentment among Panamanians for more than half a century, culminating in three days of bloody riots along the Canal Zone in January 1964. Ford, with his usual sense of even-tempered practicality, saw the issue as one of minor concern to the United States. In negotiating a peaceful resolution to the conflict over canal sovereignty, he was merely following in the footsteps of Lyndon Johnson and Richard Nixon. He also sensed that a new canal treaty could ease at least some of the persistent anti–United States sentiment in Central America.

Reagan had scored some political points over the canal as far back as the Florida primary, but the issue hit fever pitch just as the Texas campaign was unfolding, largely because of the release of congressional testimony from Ambassador Ellsworth Bunker, who headed Ford's negotiating team in Panama. Bunker revealed that Ford had ordered him to negotiate a gradual turnover of both the Canal Zone and the canal to Panama. By the time Bunker's testimony hit the newspapers, Ford had muddied the cesspool at a Dallas press conference by cryptically declaring that the United States would never relinquish its "defense right" to the canal, while blatantly evading the question of canal sovereignty.[25]

A few hours before Reagan addressed college students at the LBJ Library, he zeroed in on the Panama Canal issue during a hard-hitting speech at the Texas State Capitol. Reagan insisted that the issue went beyond symbolism, that the canal was vital to the nation's economic and military security and couldn't be trusted to Panama's military strongman Gen. Omar Torrijos, whom he commonly described as a "jerk" and a "tin-horn dictator" friend of Cuban leader Fidel Castro. Ford's evasiveness gave Reagan a second hook: the question of credibility, which had always been one of Ford's political strengths. "At the same time the president was telling Americans that he had no intentions of surrendering control of the canal, the government was negotiating the giveaway 'under the direct order of the president,'" Reagan said.[26]

Reagan's old political hero, Barry Goldwater, supported the concept of a new canal treaty and publicly suggested that Reagan let up on the issue, but to no avail. Reagan had developed a refrain whose cadence became like a song chorus you can't get out of your head, even if you want to: "We built it, we paid for it, it's ours, and we're going to keep it!" Seemingly every time he said it, the standing ovations grew more thunderous.

M. Stanton Evans, who visited Texas during the primary campaign on behalf of the American Conservative Union, recalls the unique intensity of emotion that the canal issue stirred in Texans at the time. "The Panama Canal was very big in Texas," Evans says. "Ford and Kissinger were in the process of trying to give that to Panama, and this did not sit well with a lot of conservatives, but particularly as you get closer to Panama, in Texas, it's almost a local issue there. We did some advertising there, and that was sort of the numero-uno issue for us."

The American Conservative Union's presence in the Texas campaign amounted to a small but crucial boost for Reagan, who needed any help he could get in battling the state's GOP establishment. Reagan's frustration with his situation spilled out at the state capitol when he said: "In my view, a primary belongs to the rank and file. It is for the people to tell the party structure who they want the nominee to be, not for the party structure to tell the people who their nominee will be."[27]

The American Conservative Union (ACU) had formed in 1964 as a grassroots organization espousing undiluted, free-market Goldwater conservatism. Evans, who would become ACU's chairman in 1971, had written a statement of modern conservative principles in 1960 (at the Sharon, Connecticut, home of conservative ally William F. Buckley Jr.) that the group adopted—and continues to use—as its touchstone. In that statement, Evans called capitalism "the only economic system of our time that is compatible with political liberty." He wrote that "collectivism and capitalism are incompatible," adding that "when government competes with capitalism, it jeopardizes the natural economic growth of our society and the well-being and freedom of the citizenry."

Evans had Texas roots himself. He was born in Kingsville in 1934, during a period in which his father, Medford Evans, taught at what was then known as Texas College of Arts and Industries and is now Texas A&M–Kingsville. Medford Evans was an outspoken conservative who belonged to the John Birch Society, suggested that the Civil Rights Movement was an instrument of communist subversion, and wrote a book defending the much-maligned red-baiter Joseph McCarthy.

Stanton Evans adopted his father's political views to the letter and would one day write his own book intended to rehabilitate McCarthy's reputation. A founding member of Young Americans for Freedom in the early 1960s, he was a purist who opposed incumbent president Richard Nixon in 1972 because he considered Nixon too liberal. Evans and the ACU instead endorsed insurgent

Republican challenger John Ashbrook, Evans's predecessor as ACU chairman, for president that year. As a result of such acts of impudence, the ACU did not count the leaders of the Republican Party among its loyal followers. "The Republican establishment knew we were kind of a hopeless case," Evans says. "They knew we were beyond the pale."

As the 1976 presidential race took shape, the ACU found itself with a newfound ability to impact the debate. The Supreme Court's *Buckley v. Valeo* decision in January had not only dismantled the FEC and disrupted the flow of federal campaign matching funds; it also opened the door for private organizations to spend as much money as they wanted on a political campaign, as long as their efforts were independent and not coordinated with any candidate or party.

The ACU had been a plaintiff in the *Buckley* case. Given its ideological bent, there was little doubt which candidate the organization would back in 1976. "We were very unhappy with the way Ford was running things, so we ran an independent campaign for Reagan," Evans recalls. "We kind of got our feet under us in North Carolina, and I was traveling around, state to state, and we were running radio commercials and newspaper ads on behalf of Reagan."

An independent campaign on behalf of a political candidate was a novel concept in 1976, so Evans spent a fair amount of time simply explaining to people what he was trying to accomplish. He also had to contend with suspicions from the Ford camp that the ACU secretly coordinated its efforts with Reagan's team. For Evans, who often objected to Sears's non-ideological stance, this was an ironic turn of events. "What the ACU was running was not antagonistic to but certainly different from the official Reagan campaign," he says. "We had no connection with them, and didn't agree with a lot of what was being done there. But there were people who thought I was secretly in cahoots with John Sears. So, after the fact, the FEC conducted a big investigation. They couldn't show anything, but I spent a lot of time dealing with them in November and December of '76."

In April 1976, presidential press secretary Ron Nessen complained that the ACU was throwing money around without accounting for it to the FEC, a charge that Evans hotly disputed. "We're right up to snuff and file like robots," Evans told reporters in San Antonio. The ACU's national budget for the '76 GOP primary campaign was $230,000, a fairly skimpy figure even by the standards of the time. More than $40,000 of it, however, was spent in Texas, where Evans spoke to a small gathering of fellow conservatives on the steps of the state capitol and cut radio ads extolling Reagan's virtues. "Most people didn't know who I was, but Reagan was the hook," Evans says. "Our commercials were basically just issue comparisons of the two candidates. We were kind of a fly on the wagon because we were no big source of power. We were along for the ride, but the main appeal was Reagan himself. That's what ignited the voters in Texas." Even with help from the ACU, Reagan couldn't match Ford in money or endorsements, but his Texas field generals used guerrilla tactics and blatant publicity stunts to compensate as much as they could.

When Tower decided to launch a speaking tour across the state on Ford's behalf, Barnhart and Angelo, calling themselves "The Truth Squad," set out to follow him step-for-step and counteract his message at every stop. It didn't take long for them to get under Tower's famously prickly skin. "Ray and I had a private plane to keep up with him, and we'd hold a press conference in each one of the places he went to," Angelo says. "We followed him into about three places, and he just canceled the rest of his tour. Here are two pipsqueaks going after the biggest Republican senator in the South, and we got huge publicity from it."

Barnhart and Angelo weren't the most meticulous organizers, but they were natural-born improvisers willing to walk a tightrope with the press. In at least one major case, they scheduled a media stunt before they'd even figured out what the stunt was going to be. After Reagan's early primary losses, Barnhart and Angelo agreed that they needed to shake things up, so they scheduled a press conference for Wednesday, March 17, at the state capitol. A small problem emerged: Two hours before the press conference, they still had no idea what they were going to talk about. At the last moment, they decided to use the press conference to announce that Michael Halbouty, a Texas Republican (and former Ford supporter) with a long history in the oil business, was being named the national chairman of "Oilmen for Reagan."

That solution led to another small problem: They hadn't yet cleared the idea with either Reagan or Halbouty. "It was before 8 a.m. in California, but we called over there," Angelo says. "We talked to Reagan and got approval from him for Halbouty to be announced, called Halbouty and got him to agree. And that was our press conference."

The two Texas cochairs even provided reporters with a Reagan sound bite that they had recorded over the phone that morning, with Reagan lauding Halbouty's energy expertise and saying the mustachioed oil man would be of "immense value" to the campaign. "It stunned the press, because they thought we were going to announce that we were giving up [the campaign]," Angelo says. "You'd have to say that there was an awful lot of luck involved that we were able to get ahold of Reagan and Halbouty with that short a time fuse."

Halbouty was only one of many Texas oil men who felt betrayed by Ford in December 1975, when the president signed an energy bill that slashed the oil-depletion allowance, a long-standing tax break for big oil producers. Resentment over Ford's handling of the issue hovered in the shadows of the Texas campaign, and Halbouty—a brilliant geologist and petroleum engineer who ultimately discovered more than fifty oil and gas fields in his career—was its most prominent symbol.

The Ford campaign plunked down $450,000 on the Texas race to only $250,000 for Reagan, but Angelo—along with Reagan campaign counsel Loren Smith and a Texas attorney named Jerry Smith—devised a creative way to narrow the money disparity. The plan called for Reagan delegates in the state to go out and raise funds for themselves; to literally act as though they were independent candidates campaigning for office, and not mere ballot surrogates for Reagan. "We didn't have any way to raise money statewide, and the national campaign didn't have any money," Angelo says. "So this made it possible for us to have funding for each district slate."

This strategy didn't escape the notice of the President Ford Committee, which challenged its legality and sent vague but threatening mailgrams to Reagan delegates across the state. "Your activities raise serious questions under the law and may expose you and others involved to possible criminal violations," the mailgrams warned. By this point, Loren Smith had decided that the delegate fundraising strategy violated no federal election laws, and he disregarded all complaints from the Ford camp. The Ford mailgrams complained that Reagan campaign attorneys had been alerted about the fundraising issue and replied with "a totally unresponsive and frivolous letter."[28]

During the early months of 1976, Reagan's Texas team had another innovative strategy in the works, one that involved cutting-edge technology. On February 19, 1976, Ron Dear sent a letter to John Sears, recommending that the campaign try a "test program" for a new form of marketing communications that was basically the infancy of robo-calling. A nascent Dallas company called American Telecom Network had developed a system that would make it possible to take a recording of Reagan's voice, feed it through a computer into a telephone receiver, and make thousands of calls soliciting votes and campaign contributions. The total cost of the test would only be $1,000, a pittance even for the penny-pinching Reagan campaign. Dear gushed, "Our Dallas Citizens for Reagan organization is enthusiastic about the proposal and is willing to assist. The only action on the part of the national campaign is to acquire the governor's voice on a tape recording. . . . If successful, the project might well prove significant to the national campaign."[29]

Sears never took Dear up on the idea, and it's unlikely that Reagan—who turned down a 1975 offer from CBS News to do commentaries every other night because he didn't want the TV-viewing public to burn out on him—would have embraced the concept of recorded phone solicitations at that stage of his career.

Bill Shadrach, who served as American Telecom Network's senior account executive, says the company was trying to build its name at the time by encouraging political figures to test its system. "It was a new idea, but even then we were aware of the ethical implications involved in bombing people with all these calls," Shadrach says.

While Reagan did not become the first robo-calling presidential candidate in American history, he did give his slate of Texas delegates a foolproof issue to work with. When in doubt, his delegates simply had to utter the phrase "Panama Canal," and voters started getting riled up. In retrospect, the canal controversy looks like one of those overblown obsessions that pops up regularly in presidential-election years—the same way the Taiwanese islands of Quemoy and Matsu dominated the 1960 Kennedy-Nixon debates and were soon forgotten, or the way the country went to pieces over the unspeakable injustice of Elian Gonzalez being sent back to his native Cuba but never gave the child another thought after the 2000 election cycle.

In 1977, Jimmy Carter negotiated a gradual transfer of the canal authority to Panama, and much of the outrage surrounding the issue soon evaporated. Reagan himself seemed to have moved past it by the time he assumed the presidency in 1981. But many American conservatives in 1976 longed to hear a national political figure denounce the carefully nuanced pragmatism of the Kissinger era and simply talk tough. To them, turning over the canal was an admission that the United States had taken the canal by imperialistic fiat, and they saw in Reagan a man who refused to feel guilty about any aspect of America's foreign-policy history.

"The Panama Canal issue had nothing to do with the canal," Reagan campaign lieutenant David Keene told Witcover at the time. "It said more about the American people's feelings about where the country was, and what it was powerless to do, and their frustrations about the incomprehensibility of foreign policy over the last couple of decades."[30]

CHAPTER 6

BIG JOHN'S QUANDARY

On March 10, 1976, the day after the Florida primary, Ray Barnhart paid a visit to John Connally at his downtown Houston office and asked him to endorse Reagan for president.

Barnhart didn't particularly like the former Texas governor, and he wasn't entirely convinced that a stamp of approval from this Democrat-turned-Republican would hold much sway with the GOP rank and file. But with bad news raining down in buckets on the Reagan campaign, and much of the political press suggesting that Reagan would soon withdraw from contention, Barnhart needed a bit of good publicity to counteract the gloom. "Tommy Thomas, Reagan's state chair in Florida, had been a big mouth in saying how Reagan was going to take Florida," Barnhart recalls. "And, of course, we lost ignominiously."

When Barnhart stepped into Connally's office that Wednesday morning asking for an endorsement, Big John could hardly believe what he was hearing. Barnhart recalls: "He said, 'What? He just lost!' I said, 'Yes, but if you endorse him, and he should win the nomination, you will have all the credit, because you will have saved the campaign. And if he loses, you've got nothing to lose, because you came in too late and couldn't save him.'"

That was the kind of logic a born political operator like John Connally could understand, but he wasn't buying it. Connally was accused of many things in his long political career—from his work in the late 1930s as Lyndon Johnson's congressional aide to his short tenure in the 1970s as Richard Nixon's treasury secretary—but no one ever accused him of making a sucker's bet, and gambling on Reagan in early March 1976 didn't meet anyone's definition of a good wager. Predictably, he refused Barnhart's request.

The very idea of watching the '76 campaign from the sidelines must have been galling to Connally. This, after all, was supposed to be his year. In 1972, Nixon had given serious thought to dumping Vice President Spiro Agnew from the ticket and replacing him with Connally, who had yet to officially switch his party affiliation from Democrat to Republican. Nixon's motivation was plain: to set up Connally as his heir apparent.

Although Nixon backed away from that idea, a year later he again came close to picking Connally for the number-two slot, when Agnew resigned in disgrace. In this case, a scandal-weakened Nixon soon realized that congressional Democrats would vote against Connally's confirmation because they perceived him as a serious threat for the presidency in 1976 and didn't want to put him in a prime position to make that run. As a result, Nixon went with Ford, a compromise choice that was acceptable to Democrats precisely because they knew he had no presidential aspirations and severely limited political skills.

Connally came up short for the vice presidency a third time in 1974, when Ford passed him by in favor of Nelson Rockefeller. In July 1974, a month before Ford inherited the presidency from Nixon, Connally was indicted for allegedly accepting a $10,000 bribe from milk producers in exchange for his promise to lobby the Nixon administration for higher milk-price supports. By the time Connally was acquitted of all charges, the veep window had closed. He saw Ford in the White House and surely thought, "That should be me." He saw Reagan challenging Ford and surely wondered if he should have beaten Reagan to the punch.

Tall, commanding, rugged, and given to big pronouncements, Connally was almost a stereotype of a Texas politician—like a real-life J. R. Ewing in the governor's mansion. When people called Connally a wheeler-dealer, he considered it a compliment. He was a wily political poker player whose silver fox reputation fit like a custom-made Stetson.

Connally's charisma certainly worked its magic on Nixon, whose fascination with the Floresville, Texas native could best be described as a political man-crush. Nixon once said that Connally and Nelson Rockefeller were the only two people in the United States, other than himself, who truly understood power. Notorious for bad-mouthing his cabinet members behind their backs, Nixon was never heard to utter a negative word about Connally. Connally possessed all of the same strengths Nixon had—a high political IQ, a hunger for power, an ability to quickly size people up, and a knack for manipulation—and several he wished he had: grandiosity, a near-evangelical flair for soaring oratory, and a pure physical toughness. After all, who could argue with the fact that the man had taken a bullet in Dallas in 1963 and emerged intact?

Nixon's obsessive drive to get Connally to the White House continued well after Watergate forced Nixon back into private life. Ray Hutchison recounts how Nixon, a figure whose disgraced name was carefully avoided by Republicans during the 1976 presidential race, tried—in a bizarrely covert manner—to pull strings for Connally from a distance during the '76 Republican National Convention.

> I received a mysterious call from a person who said he lived in Virginia and I'd known him a number of years earlier. He said he had a friend in New York that would like to talk to me, and asked if I'd be willing to talk to him. I had to scratch my head to figure out

who that was. It turned out that it was John Mitchell in Virginia
and the "friend in New York" was Nixon. What [Nixon] wanted
was someone who had contact with John Connally so he could get
messages to him, urging him to talk to certain people in order to
get him the nomination for vice president under President Ford.
I told him that would be doubtful, because Connally and John
Tower were not the closest of friends, and Tower was the head of
Ford's selection committee.

In 1976, Connally occupied a singularly strange position in the
Texas GOP firmament. On one hand, he was easily the biggest,
most famous figure the state party had, easily eclipsing the insu-
lar and crabby Tower. On the other hand, he'd never run for anything as a Republican, and many party activists refused to trust
him. Connally, like Bill Clinton a generation later, would often
find himself attacked for being too slick, too politically expedient
for his own good. Like Reagan, a man with whom he personally
clashed, Connally had defected from the Democratic Party and
become a Republican. But Reagan's switch just made him seem
that much more pure to conservative Republicans, because he was
a Republican by choice, not by birth. He came to the party with the
zeal of a religious convert who feels compelled to knock on doors
and spread the good news. Connally's move, by contrast, made
him look like a Machiavellian opportunist.

The distinction was crucial. Even Reagan's many detractors
knew what he believed and conceded that his views were genuine.
Even Connally's many admirers, however, occasionally wondered
if he believed in anything deeper than his own ambition.

Regardless of Connally's standing with voters, the national
media shared Nixon's fascination with him. They also knew that
Connally already had his mind set on the 1980 presidential race,
and as the '76 Texas primary approached, they watched his every

move—and nonmove—with a sense of wonder. In an April 17 syndicated column, Pat Buchanan wrote that Connally held "the high card" in the Texas primary. "Should he play his high card on behalf of one candidate, at this late hour, his intervention would never be forgotten by the other or his people," Buchanan said. "Connally is studying the situation closely, keeping his own counsel, telling friends and the press he intends to remain neutral. If he does, it will be unusual. For John Connally is a man who likes to be conspicuous in the winner's circle."[31]

That summer, on the eve of the Republican National Convention, *New York Times* columnist James Reston referred to Connally as "the most interesting ghost in the wings" of the convention: "Ford and Reagan may wreck the party temporarily with their factional wrangling, but regardless of who wins the nomination, Connally will still be around to inherit the wreckage." Reston argued that Connally represented the true future of the GOP, calling him "a political pro in a party of amateurs, a pragmatist who knows the Republicans cannot win without raiding the Democrats and Independents, a long-ball gambler and attacker in a party now very much on the defensive, and a Texan with a good chance of bringing that state into the Republican column."[32]

With so much at stake in Texas, and the primary up for grabs, both Ford and Reagan went to great lengths to court Connally. Reagan had barely stepped off the plane in Dallas for his first day of Texas campaigning when he told reporters that he was seeking Connally's support because "it would be impressive to a great many people."[33]

Even before Ford set foot in Texas, his campaign manager, Rogers Morton, found himself forced to soothe John Tower's hurt feelings over Morton's obsequious praise for Connally. In an obvious bid to flatter an endorsement out of Big John, Morton had designated him "Mr. Republican in Texas," a title that proved endlessly irritating to Tower, the GOP's only statewide officeholder. Coming into the state two days in advance of Ford, Morton slipped into damage-control mode, telling reporters at a Fort Worth press conference that he didn't mean to snub Tower. "I should have made it clear at the time that I wasn't putting Connally ahead of Tower," Morton said. "Nobody can go ahead of Tower on the list of men who have helped the Republican Party in Texas."[34]

Despite such denials, the Ford camp *was* putting Connally ahead of Tower. Tower was the good little sycophant they took for granted, while Connally was elusive and unattainable, and his determination to play hard to get just made the Ford team want him more. In the first half of April, Connally twice met with Ford at the White House, and Ford openly suggested that Big John deserved serious vice presidential consideration. On April 12, Ford appointed Ross Sterling, Connally's Houston law partner, as a US district judge. The president's decision to fill the seat so close to the Texas primary did not escape notice, especially because he hadn't previously considered the seat important enough to address in the eight months since outgoing Judge Allen B. Hannay had announced his retirement.

The biggest controversy surrounding Ford and Connally, however, involved the hints, both public and private, that a Connally endorsement for Ford might mean that the former Texas governor would be picked to replace Henry Kissinger as secretary of state after the fall election. On April 14, Rogers Morton indicated that if Connally didn't quickly decide to endorse Ford, he might lose his chance for a Cabinet appointment. "The train is leaving the station," Morton said.

This statement had the unmistakable tone of a reciprocal back-scratching deal, and Reagan seized on it as a campaign issue. At an April 15 stop in El Paso, he suggested that Ford's team may have broken the law with regard to Connally. "I am puzzled [by these reports]," Reagan said, "because my interpretation of the [federal] law is that it is illegal to offer a public office in exchange for a campaign endorsement. But who knows? Maybe the law is different for incumbents."

Ernest Angelo sensed that dangling a carrot in front of a man with Connally's ego and experience wouldn't work. He told the *Dallas Morning News* that Rogers Morton was making a "desperate attempt to bluff" Big John, adding, "Morton doesn't understand Connally. You don't bluff a guy like John Connally."[35] For his part, Tower—who had recommended Sterling for the judicial vacancy a full six months earlier but got no response from Ford until the Texas campaign was under way—had one of his aides announce that the timing of Sterling's nomination had "nothing to do with presidential politics."

Tower's assurance seemed to assure no one, least of all Nancy Reagan, who was asked about Sterling during a stop in San Antonio. In response to Ford's insistence that he'd never met Sterling and didn't know he was Connally's law partner, she cracked, "If you believe that, I've got a little swamp land in Florida I'd like to talk to you about."[36]

Given his vaunted political acumen, Connally had to realize what a dicey predicament he was in. Without question, a Ford win better served Connally's grand design. If Reagan won the nomination and carried the November election, Connally would probably be locked out of any shot at the White House for at least eight years. If Ford won the '76 election, he'd be constitutionally bound to step aside four years later.

Connally's natural inclination was to support Ford, who appeared to be running away with the national race and with whom he had a better personal relationship. At the same time, he knew that Reagan would be formidable in Texas. By supporting Ford, Connally might have ensured himself a cabinet position, but he also risked the humiliation of looking feeble in his own state if Texas voters rejected his choice. By supporting Reagan, he could look like a kingmaker, but he would also be stuck on the side of the probable convention loser and would risk criticism that he'd further divided the party. Neither of these options was likely to get Connally closer to what he wanted: the Oval Office. So he steered clear of the fray until after the primary.

One of Connally's biggest weaknesses was that he seemed to enjoy hobnobbing with the power brokers more than the masses, a tendency that Lyndon Johnson referred to when he said that Connally wasn't comfortable unless he was "in a $300 suit and the company of men wearing them." Polly Sowell, vice chair of the Texas Republican Party in 1976, was an enthusiastic Connally backer who often watched his political fortunes with frustration. "I was always anxious to turn Connally into a big plus for the Republican Party by attracting a lot of his old Democrat friends," Sowell says. "It was very hard to do, because he was very reluctant to try to get them into the Republican Party. He was a good money raiser, but I always wanted him to take some positions and do some things that would bring more Democrats into our party. But we never were able to do that. I think he didn't know how to do it."

Even with the ambivalence and distrust that Connally gener-ated among some Republicans, however, whenever he moved his charisma's dimmer switch up to maximum brightness, he could take over a room. At the 1976 Texas Republican State Convention, Connally induced an auditorium full of Reagan diehards to give him a standing ovation when he used his keynote address to lobby for federal term limits. He also used the state convention to assure the media that he had no interest in the vice presidency, which he called "the worst job in the world."

Despite such disavowals, Sowell remembers talking to Connally that summer and getting the sense that he would have gladly accepted the veep offer from Ford.

> I was crazy about John Connally and he was working to be vice president, so I was trying to help him do that. There were several of us who went to the Kansas City convention with the purpose of getting Connally on the ticket. That was our mission, and, of course, we failed. We went around and talked about Connally with people from other states, but, of course, the only person to make that decision was President Ford himself. We were never able to meet with him, and I don't know that we even asked.

That fall, Hutchison got a firsthand look at the animosity that existed at the time between Connally and Reagan, who were both eyeing the 1980 GOP nomination from afar. Reagan was making a Texas campaign swing on behalf of Ford, flying from Longview to a Houston fundraiser hosted by Connally. Nancy Reagan sat in the chartered plane, reading a magazine article about the Reagans' ranch in Santa Barbara, California, when she abruptly lifted her head and shouted to her husband: "Have you seen this?" Nancy proceeded to read a quote from Connally suggesting that the Reagans' 688-acre spread hardly qualified as a ranch.

"At that point, she asked us where the plane was heading, and we told her we were going to Houston," Hutchison says. "She asked, 'Is Connally going to be there?' I said, 'Well, as a matter of fact he is. He is going to be the master of ceremonies for this rather massive campaign event.' So she said, 'Turn this airplane around!' Finally, Governor Reagan intervened and said, 'No, we should keep on going.'"

Ronald Reagan did manage, however, to get some thinly veiled revenge against the man who'd denigrated his beloved Rancho del Cielo. "Everybody referred to Connally as Big John, and many people considered that nickname a negative," Hutchison says. "Reagan certainly considered it a negative. So, throughout his speech, he continually referred to Connally as 'Big John.'"

Just to prove that his wheeler-dealer reputation was more than media-concocted myth, Connally somehow found a way during the April 1976 primary campaign to insert himself into the state's other big story that month: the deepening mystery behind Howard Hughes's will. On Tuesday, April 27, Connally was on the twenty-fifth floor of a Mormon office building in Salt Lake City approximately three hours before a purported Hughes will mysteriously popped up on the same floor of the building in an unstamped envelope. Connally, who was director of a Texas banking conglomerate at the time, had called a meeting with Mormon leaders to discuss a project of mutual interest.

Connally was never tied to the mysterious will, but it remained part of the enduring Connally puzzle, alongside the single-bullet theory in Dallas, the milk-fund scandal, and the question of how a politician so driven, well-connected, and magnetic didn't make it to the White House.

Connally understood, better than most of his peers did, that politics is all about timing. If you miss your golden opportunity, it might not come around again. In the summer of 1973, it would have been easy to look ahead to 1976 and predict a general-election matchup between Connally and Ted Kennedy. As it turned out, neither man even entered the race. Kennedy sensed that 1976 was his year, a rare moment when no obvious, high-profile Democratic rivals were lined up in his path. But with his family life in turmoil, he reluctantly passed. Four years later, when he finally made the big leap, he faced the daunting challenge of knocking off a president from his own party (Carter), and failed miserably.

Unlike Kennedy, Connally was stymied in '76 not by a failure of nerve, but by Watergate's political body count. The resignation of Nixon and the milk-fund indictment had thrown everything out of whack for him. Like Kennedy, Connally would try to make the planets align again in 1980, but they refused to cooperate.

CHAPTER 7
ONE-PARTY STATE OF MIND

Jim Lunz became a Republican by accident. In 1959, Lunz moved from Austin to San Antonio to pursue a real estate deal that went belly-up almost as quickly as he could unpack his bags. Over the next few months of messy legal travails, Lunz became such a constant presence at his lawyer's office that the attorney started thinking of ways to get rid of him.

One idea he came up with was to encourage Lunz to talk to the Bexar County Republican Party chairman about possibly helping to administer the 1960 US Census. (Because Republican Dwight Eisenhower was president at the time, most 1960 census jobs came via GOP patronage.) Shortly after the census was completed, the county chairman asked Lunz if he would manage the campaigns of some Republican legislative candidates from the area. Lunz didn't have anything better to do, so he said yes.

Fortunately for Lunz, the job of a Republican campaign manager in Texas at that time didn't come with much pressure. From the beginning, you knew you were going to lose, so you just tried to make it as competitive as you could. One of the biggest challenges for the Texas GOP was simply *finding* candidates, preferably those with a little spare cash and an ability to accept defeat with stoic grace. "In those days, the state was not paying for the primary election, so you paid for the primary out of the $300 candidate filing fees," says Lunz, a veteran GOP organizer and campaign manager. "To get candidates on the ballot, you had to find somebody that wanted to commit suicide and that was willing to pay for it themselves. So there weren't many people anxious to participate in the Republican primary. And we hadn't progressed that far by 1976."

There are multiple ways to illustrate the Democratic Party's longtime control of Texas politics. In 1954, the state's entire twenty-four-member congressional delegation was Democratic; in 1960, only two of the more than five thousand elected officials in the state—from constables up to US senators—were Republicans; in 1966, only ten years before the Reagan-Ford duel, 180 of the 181 members of the Texas legislature were Democrats.

But no single trivia item so forcefully conveys what an utter nonentity the post-Reconstruction GOP was in Texas than this tidbit from 1912: That year, Socialist Party presidential candidate Eugene Debs came within a whisker of drawing more Texas votes than incumbent Republican President William Howard Taft, with Taft at 9 percent and Debs at 8 percent. (Granted, Taft faced dissension within the GOP ranks over the Bull Moose Party challenge of his mentor-turned-adversary, Theodore Roosevelt, but this was hardly the look of a so-called major party.) At times such as those, the state GOP had to fight simply to be recognized as the biggest cipher on the block. You couldn't say that the Texas Republican Party of the 1950s and 1960s was a shambles, because it really didn't have enough individual pieces to constitute a shambles. It was the irrelevant, all-but-silent opposition. Throwing their votes away was an intramural sport for Republicans. "The only time we'd have a Republican sitting in the legislature would be if they had a special election, and we'd elect somebody to fill out a term and they'd get defeated in the next general election," Lunz recalls.

Prior to 1962, the Texas GOP didn't even bother holding primary elections, generally choosing their nominees at county and states caucuses. Once the GOP primary became a fact of life, the party not only had to find candidates willing to pay the filing fees, they had to contend with the fact that the Democrats who ran Texas politics refused to provide them with voting machines. As late as the '76 primary contest between Ford and Reagan, Republicans in 44 of the state's 254 counties could not vote because no polling booths were available for them.

Texas Republicans occasionally had to go to absurd lengths just to hold a primary. In 1962, Arkansas County chairwoman Shirley Dimmick vainly struggled to find an available facility for a GOP primary. She asked Democrats in her hometown of Rockport if they would share their voting facilities with the GOP. After being turned down and waking up one morning to find five dead rattlesnakes and a sign reading "No Two-Party" hanging on her fence, Dimmick defiantly held the county's first-ever Republican primary under the shade of an oak tree.[37]

Shirley Green was a young mother of two living in Austin in 1960. Partly out of a "craving for adult companionship," she volunteered to help out at the local Nixon headquarters. Four years later, Green, who would go on to work as deputy press secretary for George H. W. Bush during his first term as vice president and special assistant for presidential messages and correspondence during his presidency, was recruited by her fellow Republicans to run for state representative, just to have a GOP name on the ballot. "The state Republican Party encouraged the county parties to file as many candidates as they could for local offices, so that everybody wouldn't be out there campaigning for [Lyndon] Johnson, who was already stronger than onions," Green says, in a husky Lone Star twang.

Like many of her GOP colleagues at the time, Green accepted

her electoral suicide mission with no misgivings. "The good thing about that kind of campaign is that your heart isn't going to be broken, because you never expected to win," she says. "It was just a matter of trying to help the party and doing a little better than we did two years before. But it was tough, and only people that were willing to take the guff, and didn't have their egos wrapped up in it, would do it."

Women played a crucial role in the Texas GOP's slow emergence from the weedy underbrush, a fact that Green chalks up to the fear that many men felt about bucking the Democratic power structure at a time when the axis of Johnson in the White House and a pre-Republican Connally in the governor's mansion controlled the state. "I talked to a friend who was with an ad agency, asking if he would help place my television commercials when I was able to raise enough money to run a few campaign ads," Green recalls. "He said, 'Of course, I'll be happy to.' When it actually came time to do it, he called and said, 'Shirley, I can't. My bosses won't allow us to help any of the Republican candidates.' That's the kind of climate there was in the business community. It was too risky for their careers."

As early as the 1950s, the Dems' uneasy coalition of Dixiecrat conservatives and New Deal liberals had shown signs of fraying in presidential general-election contests, with Dwight Eisenhower twice carrying the state over liberal Democrat Adlai Stevenson. In 1952, Texas governor Allan Shivers, a hard-nosed conservative Democrat, endorsed Eisenhower, causing a near-revolt from angry Texas progressives.

With his loud insistence on the primacy of states' rights, Shivers was something of an ideological precursor to Rick Perry. In fact, he rejected Stevenson largely over a single-issue spat that concerned states' rights: Shivers argued that the federal government should not be allowed to seize oil-bearing tidelands in the Gulf of

Mexico and that the territory should be controlled by the state of Texas. Eisenhower took the states'-rights position, while Stevenson favored federal control. That was all Shivers needed to know.

By that point, the Texas legislature (with Shivers's blessing) had passed a law allowing both major parties to nominate the same candidates. As a result, Shivers and every other statewide office holder, with the exception of Agriculture Commissioner John White, accepted the nominations of both parties in 1952. In a way, this strange move was an acknowledgment of the fact that the Texas GOP struggled just to get names on the ballot. If the Republican Party couldn't generate its own candidates, Shivers and his fellow Democrats would gladly double-dip and run against themselves. On a deeper level, however, this amounted to treasonous activity from wavering Democrats. Predictably enough, the hard feelings between Shivercrats and party liberals went both ways. In both 1952 and 1956, Shivers had to fight just to get seated at the Democratic National Convention.

Like many 1950s conservatives south of the Mason-Dixon line, Shivers often used states' rights as a shield for his stubborn segregationist views. Sometimes he didn't bother to hide his motives. His 1957 gubernatorial farewell address to the legislature included a plea to his fellow Texans that whites and African Americans continue to be kept apart.

The state party's 1952 split over the presidential race was an early indicator of problems to come, but at the same time it was also an aberration driven by Eisenhower's unique status as the nation's most admired war hero. After Eisenhower, no Republican presidential candidate carried Texas until Nixon in '72 (although Nixon came close in both '60 and '68), and given that he carried every state but Massachusetts in that election, his Texas triumph didn't prove too much. That same year, Republican Hank Grover came close to knocking off Dolph Briscoe in the gubernatorial election, another sign that conservative Democrats would consider bolting for a particular candidate who spoke their language.

In 1966 and 1972, liberal Democrats helped John Tower win reelection to the Senate as a protest vote against conservative Democratic nominees. In the case of the liberal Democrats, they were simply making mischief to express their frustration with the Democratic power structure. Deep down, they knew they had nowhere else to go. Grover's strong gubernatorial showing was more telling because he ran a populist conservative campaign, against the play-it-safe advice of Tower, and was able to pry loose some conservative Democratic votes.

For the most part, however, conservative Democrats held so much power in the state they felt little motivation to stray from their party. In fact, despite all the public backbiting between the two factions, conservative and liberal Democrats often found their relationship to be a symbiotic one. Babe Schwartz says: "We were liberals who benefited from people voting the straight Democratic ticket. The conservatives ran the show anyway, so they didn't mind. We used our minority power in the Senate to act, in some cases, as a silver bullet. For conservatives, having that cover as a Democrat allowed them to function and be where the power was."

The historical effect of the Democratic Party's fragile coalition in Texas—and in much of the Deep South—was that it tended to pull major political figures to the center. Lloyd Bentsen may have been a fiscal conservative and a defense hawk, but he also carefully cultivated his relationships with labor in Texas because he wanted to hold the party's broad base together.

Lyndon Johnson carried all of the party's contradictions within his tortured political soul: making it to Congress as a liberal New Dealer at the height of Franklin Roosevelt's popularity; pandering to the extreme, segregationist right to beat former governor Coke Stevenson in the much-disputed 1948 senatorial election; and ultimately, as president, putting all his political capital on the table to get the historic Civil Rights Act through Congress in 1964. For much of his career, Johnson was identified as a conservative Democrat, yet his presidency ushered in the most ambitious, liberal set of social programs since FDR.

The realignment that Reagan sparked in 1976 sent conservatives scurrying from the Democratic Party to the GOP and left moderate and liberal Republicans looking for a home. As a result, Texas conservatives no longer had to pay lip service to liberal concerns, and liberals no longer had the protective cover of the Democratic Party's all-powerful coalition. Post-Reagan, the parties, which had always been divided by history, tradition, and socioeconomic factors, would be split more firmly than ever before along ideological lines.

The pre-Reagan political landscape in the Lone Star State was dissected in a January 1973 episode of William F. Buckley's PBS series, *Firing Line*. On that show, Republican leader Beryl Milburn unhappily conceded that the "tradition of Texas is to participate in the Democratic primary," adding, "I don't think it's going to change anytime soon."

Buckley saw the problem as a catch-22 for Texas Republicans: They couldn't elect more officeholders unless they could stimulate more participation in their primaries, but they couldn't get people interested in their primaries because they had so few officeholders. "If you have a tradition in the state that has lasted almost 100 years of electing only a Democratic governor," Buckley said, "it seems to me that in order to participate at all in the activities of that state, a Republican is almost driven to participate in the Democratic primary."[38]

The Texas GOP received a small but lasting boost in the early 1970s from a series of court rulings (*Graves v. Barnes, White v. Regester*) that dismantled the state's long-established use of at-large and multimember voting districts. These multimember districts had been designed to suppress the voting power of African Americans in large urban areas such as Houston and Dallas, and Mexican Americans in San Antonio and other parts of South Texas.

The court-enforced conversion to single-member districts created new possibilities for minorities in the Democratic Party, but they also gave hope to long-suffering Republicans. The Texas GOP benefited because single-member districts prevented Democrats from diluting the power of the Republican Party in pockets where its voters were concentrated. Buoyed by these changes, the Texas GOP had managed to inch its way forward over the first half of the '70s, growing from 10 members in the 181-member Texas legislature to 21—a total that was still anemic but represented an increase of more than 100 percent—in a span of four years.

But the long, drawn-out Watergate scandal had devastated the party's national base to such a degree that some political observers openly speculated that the GOP might be finished as a major political party in the United States. Reagan himself alluded to this concern when he told the assembled delegates at the 1976 Republican National Convention, "We may be fewer in numbers than we've ever been."

The gap between the liberals who controlled much of the Democratic agenda at the federal level and the conservatives who ran the Democratic Party at the state level created some moments of dissonance for Texas Democrats, to be sure. That's why many Texas Democrats rejected party presidential nominee George McGovern in 1972 in favor of Nixon. But conservative Texas Democrats had little trouble finding candidates they liked in primaries, and few of them would have considered wasting their vote on a Republican primary.

That's why the Bentsen Primary Bill and Reagan's presence in the '76 race were so pivotal to the Texas GOP. In 1976, for the first time in its history, the party could offer a primary election that was something more than a slate of candidates competing to be November sacrificial lambs. They had a competitive presidential contest with a charismatic, bona-fide conservative beckoning Democrats to defect, as Reagan himself had done nearly a generation earlier. Pulling George Wallace Democrats away from their party's primary and into the GOP fold meant a chance to change their allegiance for good.

Barbara Staff was one of many former Democrats electrified by Reagan's candidacy. A native of the Fort Worth suburb of Cleburne, Staff grew up in a family of New Deal Democrats. In 1970, at the age of forty-five, she took a political science class at the University of North Texas and found herself annoyed with what she considered to be the America-bashing message of her liberal professor. That same year, she put her newfound political consciousness to work for Jim Collins, a Republican congressman from Dallas. "When I first became a Republican, I think we could have met in a phone booth, there were so few of us," Staff recalls. "It really did have an elitist reputation among most of my friends. Most of my friends were Democrats, and my family members thought I was backslidin' when I said I was going to work for the Republicans. My gosh, they worshipped [Franklin Delano] Roosevelt like I worshipped Reagan."

Staff's husband, Bill, a transplant from Washington State, worked for Magnolia Petroleum before starting his own forensic consulting business called Haag Engineering. He was thoroughly apolitical. "He said, 'Honey, I'll do the business, you do the politics.' And that was a good arrangement," she says.

Feisty and irrepressibly blunt, Staff never hesitated to blast any Republican she perceived as insufficiently in tune with her conservative principles. At the December 1975 Southern Republican Leadership Conference in Austin, with the likes of Tower, Connally, and Ford cabinet members Earl Butz and William Simon in attendance, she blasted the president for surrounding himself with "liberal advisers."

Nearly thirty years removed from her last political battle, Staff—who lives in a gated community in the affluent North Texas town of Plano—retains much of her old resentment against Tower for his support of Ford, and she can't resist zinging him for his legendary reputation as a philanderer. "What a travesty he was," she says. "My dealings were mostly with his aides because when I tried to set up something, I never could reach little mighty John. Even his aides didn't like him. One of them told me that his primary responsibility was, in the case of a fire alarm at a hotel, to get the woman out of Tower's room."

Staff doesn't hold Reagan's kids in much higher esteem. She recalls that Maureen Reagan canceled out of a speaking engagement at a big Dallas Country Club fundraising breakfast at the last minute and says his kids made a habit of pulling no-shows at campaign events. "I do not have any respect for any of his children," she says. "We just had a lot of difficulty with them in the campaign. Anytime you'd want to use them, something invariably happened."

Staff endured such letdowns because of her overwhelming admiration for Reagan himself. She remembers meeting him at DFW Airport after Jimmy Lyon had invited the former California governor for a visit with some of his prospective campaign workers. They talked for about twenty minutes, with Reagan apparently sizing up Staff to assess if she could be of help to his campaign. She spent most of the conversation trying to shake off a powerful case of hero worship. "I was thunderstruck," Staff says. "It was the second coming."

Many Texas Republicans admired Reagan personally and shared his belief system, but nonetheless resented him for splitting the party at a time when it was already weakened by Watergate. "I thought Ford had done a wonderful job in a short period of time," Green says. "I admired him as such a straightforward, good man that I thought it was unnecessarily divisive to have a contested primary. Because we knew that when a sitting president is challenged within his own party, chances are great he won't win the general election. So I was very, very unhappy that Reagan chose to run against Ford."

Steve Heinrich had grown up on the East Side of San Antonio and spent his afternoons helping out at his parents' grocery store. Every afternoon at 6 p.m., a half hour before closing time, Heinrich and his parents would tune in to AM news radio for one Reagan's syndicated three-minute radio commentaries, in which he would lay out the conservative case on issues ranging from public-sector employee strikes to government regulation of the pharmaceutical industry. Reagan, at the suggestion of his old Hollywood acting friend, Efrem Zimbalist Jr., had launched his radio series immediately after leaving the California governor's mansion in January 1975. "He was so good at picking an example that extrapolated to the big picture," Heinrich remembers. "My parents loved listening to it. So we were fans of Ronald Reagan."

When Heinrich, one of Bexar County's most dedicated young GOP activists at the time, had to choose sides in the 1976 presidential race, however, he picked Ford. "I was torn between the two," he says. "I always liked Jerry Ford myself, but Reagan appealed to us politically. But a lot of it was the fact that it's really, really hard to knock a sitting president off in your primary and win in November. And we were better off electing Ford than Jimmy Carter."

Despite his misgivings about Reagan's primary challenge, Heinrich might have been tempted to join the Reagan team if they'd made the effort to recruit him. He never heard from any Reagan campaign representatives, however, so when old friend Shirley Green, the Bexar County chair for the President Ford Committee, asked him to join Ford's team, he immediately accepted.

Comparing the zealous Reagan 76ers to current Tea Party activists, Heinrich says the Reagan army demanded a level of ideological purity that many Republicans at the time found hard to maintain. "It was an odd collection of disparate people who were just unhappy with what the government was doing," Heinrich says. "They didn't think that we were right-wing enough. We used to laughingly refer to them as the Reagan Crazies." Unfortunately for the Ford camp, the "Reagan Crazies" started growing in numbers as both the campaign and the Texas weather heated up in April.

Reagan had fared poorly with senior citizens early in the primary season, in part because some seniors worried that his zeal for budget slashing might extend to Medicare, and possibly because Ford, as a known quantity, seemed less threatening and more reassuring. Staff, however, actively pursued the North Texas senior vote, working nursing homes and senior centers with regularity. "I didn't even think in terms of Democrats or Republicans," she says. "I was just looking for conservatives. Within my book club or my bridge groups, I could sort out conservative people, and they were the people that I talked to, because I didn't care what party they belonged to. I knew that Reagan's message of small government was going to get to them."

CHAPTER 8

★ THE GREAT TAMALE INCIDENT

Gerald Ford's aides liked to say that Ford was the most athletic man ever to reside in the White House. The empirical evidence certainly backed them up. An All-American center who played on two University of Michigan national-championship football teams and turned down NFL contract offers from both the Detroit Lions and Green Bay Packers, Ford's sports accomplishments had no precedent in the Oval Office. Only Theodore Roosevelt, the vaunted outdoorsman with an unquenchable drive to prove himself in every imaginable form of athletic competition, came close.

Unfortunately for Ford, this message never really translated to the American people. Few people ever saw archival footage of Ford on the football field, but the whole world saw him—in an endless loop of prime-time network-news coverage—tumble down the steps of Air Force One as he arrived for a state visit in Salzburg, Austria. They all heard about him bonking a woman in the head with an errant golf shot. And, of course, they all saw Chevy Chase impersonate Ford—without making the slightest effort to look or sound like him—on *Saturday Night Live* simply by depicting him as the clumsiest, most discombobulated oaf to ever walk the face of the earth.

Ford's defenders to this day argue that his presidential mishaps were attributable not to an innate clumsiness, but to a torn ACL in his knee that he'd suffered at Michigan and never had repaired. Once the image took over, however, the stories proliferated faster than he could laugh them off. One of the most embarrassing incidents, which happened on the first day of his 1976 Texas campaign swing, suggested that Mexican cuisine, much like aircraft staircases, was an adventure for the president at that stage of his life.

On the morning of Friday, April 9, Ford flew from Andrews Air Force Base in Maryland to San Antonio, accompanied by Chief of Staff Dick Cheney, Press Secretary Ron Nessen, and the ever-loyal John Tower. Ford had just come off big primary wins that week in Wisconsin and New York and sensed that he was on the verge of knocking Reagan out of the race, though he cautiously described himself as an "underdog" in Texas.

After greeting Ray Hutchison, San Antonio mayor Lila Cockrell, and a host of military officials at Kelly Air Force Base, Ford and his motorcade headed out to his first big campaign event in Texas: a midday reception at the Alamo, hosted by the San Antonio chapter of the Daughters of the Republic of Texas (DRT). As soon as Ford, Tower, and Cockrell entered the Alamo grounds, they were greeted by a DRT hospitality table.

The particulars of what happened next have slipped into the South Texas urban-legend category, but this is how Cockrell gingerly recounts it: "It was kind of a garden setting. They had beverages and some tamales. It was very quickly evident that President Ford was not very familiar with tamales. It was noticed that he appeared about to try to eat a tamale with the shuck on. So it was explained to him that you remove the shuck." News accounts of the time—and since then, for that matter—all described a baffled president, in plain sight of reporters and more than two hundred guests, biting into a tamale without first removing its nonedible corn husk. The implication was that stunned DRT members had practically saved him from choking on his own cultural ignorance.

A picture from the Alamo event that appeared in the *San Antonio Express-News* showed a bug-eyed Ford, leaning forward and looking like he was in the middle of gulping something painful. Although the caption pointed out that the "odd grimace" captured in the photo happened well after his "unfortunate experience" with the tamale, the image stuck. A column in the newspaper also noted that the face of one DRT member was "frozen into a picture of sheer disbelief when President Ford bit down on that tamale."

All these years later, Cockrell still makes the aural equivalent of a cringe whenever the subject comes up, probably because it pains her to be reminded that a presidential visit she hosted resulted in ridicule for the president. That may or may not factor in her memory of that day, but in any event, her version of the story is less dramatic than the one told by media eyewitnesses. "My recollection is that it looked as if he were about to [take a bite], but didn't actually do it," she says. "When it happened, he didn't have much of a response. It was all pretty low-key and no one wished to cause him any embarrassment."

Arthur Troilo, a San Antonio attorney who'd accepted John Tower's request to be South Texas regional coordinator for the Ford campaign, said the tamale incident completely escaped his attention until the press picked up on it. "I was in the front rows of the crowd in front of the Alamo, but nobody noticed anything," he says. "But the reporters caught it."

Ford moved on to a gathering at the Hilton Palacio del Rio Hotel along the San Antonio Riverwalk, where he greeted local campaign workers and received an oil painting of Abraham Lincoln from Fernando Cortez, San Antonio's officially designated bicentennial artist. From there he spoke to two hundred President Ford Committee staffers and volunteers at the San Antonio Convention Center after an enthusiastic introduction from Troilo. By all accounts, Ford was in good spirits and oblivious to the commotion his Alamo visit would soon cause.

For all the inherent silliness of the tamale gaffe, it played into some chronic, dead-serious problems for Ford's candidacy. His image as a bumbler consistently threatened to negate any prestige points he gained from the trappings of the presidency. Voters might be impressed to see the majestic Air Force One land at their local airport, but at the same time, its presence would offer a reminder of the time Ford took the express route down the steps. The site of the Marine One helicopter landing on the White House South Lawn inevitably carried memories of Ford repeatedly bumping his head on the doorway. All the positive campaign work he did in San Antonio on April 9 was soon forgotten, but the tamale incident lingered. "When I saw the stories, I thought, 'This is just so typical of the way he was being covered,'" Cockrell says. "It seemed that the media, for whatever reason, was not focusing on the content, but if it was any little misstep, or something that was peripheral, that was what got the attention."

Given the scope of the Latino vote in South Texas, it also did Ford no favors to leave Chicanos with the memory of an American president nearly choking on Mexican food because he didn't know how to eat it properly. It didn't rankle on the same scale as Jimmy Carter's infamous 1979 quip that he'd suffered a bout of "Montezuma's Revenge" during a diplomatic trip to Mexico, but it certainly wasn't ideal primary-campaign spin control.

John Knaggs, a longtime GOP operative who worked on all of Tower's successful senate campaigns, wrote in his 1986 book, *Two-Party Texas*, that Ford's Mexican American supporters were "crestfallen" over the tamale incident because it provided evidence that "the candidate from Michigan knew little about Spanish-Mexican culture of the Southwest."

These kinds of misadventures seemed to follow Ford around during the Texas campaign, and Reagan partisans could barely stifle their amusement. In Longview, the Kilgore Rangerettes performed a routine for Ford on the runway of Gregg County Airport. Clad in their classic white cowgirl hats, western outfits, and knee-high white boots, the famous drill team lined up to greet the president when he arrived. As he walked down the line, Ford swung his left arm and knocked a hat off the Rangerette on his left. Before she could pick it up, he swung his right arm and knocked the hat off the Rangerette on his right.

Sometimes, he just seemed snakebit. Back in Washington, even a routine photo op took a strange turn when Tawny Godin, Miss America 1976, dropped by the White House for a brief Rose Garden visit with Ford but was chased away by a swarm of bees. "We were really concerned about Ford's first trip to Texas after we got going," Angelo says with a laugh. "After the tamale thing, we weren't too worried."

Ford's pratfalls, gaffes, and gastronomic miscues were surely embarrassing, but did they actually have an impact on his standing with voters? The evidence was fairly ambiguous. Unquestionably, the single biggest factor in Ford's approval ratings was his controversial pardon of Nixon on September 8, 1974. A Gallup poll taken September 6–9, 1974, found that Ford's approval rating was at a robust 66 percent. Three weeks later, only 50 percent of the American public approved of his performance. His popularity never fully rebounded from that setback.

In May 1975, however, Ford experienced a minor political surge after he ordered a military operation to rescue the crew of the SS *Mayaguez*, a US ship seized by Cambodian forces. By the beginning of June, his popular approval had jumped from 40 to 51 percent. That same month, however, he made his infamous fall from the steps of Air Force One as he arrived in Salzburg. Coincidentally or not, by the beginning of August he had sagged back to 45 percent and never made it back over 50 percent before the November 1976 general election.

Another clue comes from Gallup's annual "most admired man" poll. Gallup started the poll in 1946, and almost every year since then, respondents have picked the president of the United States as their most admired man. Dwight Eisenhower earned this distinction nine years in a row, while both Lyndon Johnson and Richard Nixon won four years in a row. In 1998, at the height of the Monica Lewinsky sex scandal, Bill Clinton was nonetheless selected as America's most admired man. The only sitting president in the history of the poll never to be named "most admired" is Gerald Ford. Ford was neither the only "accidental" president in the history of the poll (the same could be said for Harry Truman and Lyndon Johnson) nor the only chief executive to find himself turning into a political piñata. Certainly, every president between Truman and Barack Obama has been subjected to withering attacks, but most of these criticisms were rooted in policy decisions or ethical behavior. Ford, however, received a highly personal brand of ridicule that inevitably chipped away at whatever respect the American public had for him when he took office. At the very least, his blunders diverted media attention away from his best efforts to look presidential.

Five hours after his ill-fated Alamo visit, Ford landed in Dallas's Love Field and held a short press conference. "I don't know if we can win [Texas] without Connally's support," Ford said. "We will work very hard."[39]

Pushing hard to prove his conservative credentials, Ford

railed against big government during an economic briefing at the Fairmount Hotel attended by nearly two thousand people. He blasted the $8 billion annual cost of the federal food-stamps program and said it needed to be slashed. He bragged that he'd rejected costly spending proposals from congressional Democrats because they were the "wrong medicine" for an economy regaining its vitality a year after the most brutal recession the nation had suffered since the 1930s. "Common sense told me the right method was to stimulate growth in the private sector," Ford said.[40]

After the briefing, Ford went upstairs to the Gold Room for a cocktails-and-hors-d'oeuvres fundraiser with 250 Texas business leaders, including powerful Dallas real estate mogul Trammell Crow, his state finance chairman. From there, Ford and Tower rushed to Arlington Stadium so the president could throw out the first ball of the Texas Rangers' 1976 home opener against the Minnesota Twins.

After sitting through one inning of the game, they motored to Texas Stadium for a Law Day dinner hosted by the Irving Bar Association. Only three months earlier, the Dallas Cowboys had made their third Super Bowl appearance in six years. They essentially ruled the Texas sports world, so Ford was only too happy when Cowboys defensive linemen Ed "Too Tall" Jones and Harvey Martin presented him with a team jersey. (Cowboys head coach Tom Landry openly supported Ford in the primary and appeared with him at a Dallas reception later in the month.)

For Ford, it had been a long, frenetic day that began in the White House, ended in Dallas, and included at least seven campaign events—plus an airport press conference—along the way. His overnight stay at the Fairmont Hotel alone ran up a campaign bill of $25,000, much of it to pay pastry chef Gerd Lunkowski for the days of work he put into whittling four Republican elephants of white chocolate and sculpting a two-foot-tall chocolate cowboy riding a pair of skis, all for Ford's Dallas fundraising reception.

Everywhere he went, Ford was warmly received, but it was impossible to determine whether all his activity had done the campaign any good. In fact, judging from the snickers he generated after the tamale incident, it's possible that the opposite happened. Bob Teeter, Ford's pollster, determined over the course of the primaries that whenever Ford made campaign appearances, his national poll numbers dropped. Three months after the Texas primary, as Ford prepared for the Republican National Convention, Spencer stepped into the Oval Office and gave Ford this dose of political tough love: "Mr. President, as a campaigner, you're no fucking good."[41]

Even before Spencer stunned him with that blunt message, Ford knew that he couldn't match Reagan as a stump speaker or match his credibility with the state's right-wingers, so he framed the primary as a choice between substance and superficiality, between diplomacy and demagoguery, between sober, pragmatic leadership and wild irresponsibility. In a five-minute Texas commercial featuring John Tower, Ford was presented as a calm, patient, fatherly man of reason, with still photos showing him listening intently at Cabinet meetings, always holding a pipe in his hand. It was like having Ward Cleaver in the White House. "Some who seek the presidency have not fared as well," the commercial's narrator intoned, leaving little doubt as to the identity of at least one of these presidential seekers. "In losing, they have fallen back on an ill-considered and perilously superficial message. They have made pronouncements about national defense that are both shallow and misinformed." The commercial also suggested that certain unnamed president contenders needed to be careful to "not use words bristling with impatience or indulge in careless saber rattling." A thirty-second Texas spot condensed that message, with Tower staring straight into the camera and saying, "I urge you to vote for the responsible man."

This fear-the-warmonger advertising strategy had worked brilliantly for Lyndon Johnson in 1964 against Barry Goldwater, but this was a different year and a primary rather than a general election. More importantly, Ford was not Johnson, and Reagan was not Goldwater. A message of moderation coming from an imposing, larger-than-life presence like Johnson—in an election year when the nation's grief over the assassination of John Kennedy provided the sitting president with an extra measure of public goodwill— might have seemed prudent in 1964, but it had the ring of bland weakness to many Texas Republicans in 1976.

Taken together, Ford's commercials and stump speeches tried to split the difference between Reagan and Carter. At a Houston press conference, he described himself as "conservative enough to win the Texas primary and middle-of-the-road enough to win the election in November."[42] This recalled Richard Nixon's old advice that GOP candidates should run to the right during the primaries and run to the center for the general election. Nixon never advised, however, that candidates telegraph their punches well before they've locked down the nomination, as Ford made the mistake of doing in Houston.

Ford's point to Texas Republicans was that he was more electable than Reagan because Reagan's base—while undeniably rabid—was extremely narrow. Ford's Texas newspaper ads not only categorized his unnamed opponent as reckless; they insisted that Ford, unlike Reagan, could beat the Democratic nominee: "If you want to vote for the man who has experience, proven leadership and responsibility on his side . . . the man who can win next November . . . that man is Gerald Ford."

Given the soft nature of Ford's support, electability was a sound plank on which to attract GOP voters. It basically told Texas Republicans, "Think with your head, not with your heart, and take the most conservative candidate who can actually win." Ford partisans, with some justification, looked at Reagan and saw Barry Goldwater with a Hollywood smile. If Goldwater had scared away independents only twelve years earlier, Reagan might lead the GOP into the same trap. Electability arguments, however, only work if voters believe them, and when Texas Republicans sized up Reagan and Ford, they weren't so easily convinced that the charisma-deficient Ford offered the GOP its best shot at victory in November.

Whatever Ford lacked in pure panache and quotability, his wife Betty more than made up for. A former dancer who had already married and divorced before her 1947 introduction to a young congressional hopeful from Grand Rapids named Jerry Ford, Betty reveled in the spotlight in a way that no American First Lady had since Eleanor Roosevelt. Even more than Eleanor Roosevelt, however, she was willing to risk the disapproval of her husband's political base: emphatically declaring her support for the Equal Right Amendment, calling the Supreme Court's decision to legalize abortion "the best thing in the world," suggesting that marijuana use was no big deal, and publicly stating that she wouldn't be surprised if her teenage daughter Susan came to her with the news that she was having an affair. That final remark stirred W. A. Criswell, pastor of the First Baptist Church of Dallas, to decry her "gutter mentality."

If her candor made her a pariah to social conservatives, it also won her the admiration of feminists and liberal Democrats who would have never considered voting for Gerald Ford. Her public battle with breast cancer (she was diagnosed a month after becoming First Lady) only intensified that bond. As Ford traveled around the country in early '76 stumping for votes, he was often greeted by supporters holding signs with the following message: "Vote for Betty's Husband."

Betty Ford had never been to Texas before the 1976 primary, but she made a high-impact debut in the state during San Antonio's annual Fiesta celebration, an homage to the Texas war for independence that is always the biggest blowout of the year in the Alamo City. Acting as grand marshal of the River Fiesta Parade, the First Lady—described rather quaintly by the *San Antonio Express-News* as a "slender, attractive woman"—sailed down the San Antonio River in a gold-and-white, eagle-decorated barge covered in Plexiglas, all the while clutching a bouquet of yellow roses.

During her stop, she autographed a *guitarron* and *vihuela* for two local mariachi musicians, visited a family with one-year-old quadruplets, and blithely handled every question the press threw at her. Yes, she said, she would resume her active campaigning on behalf of the Equal Rights Amendment once this presidential-election business was sorted out. No, the president doesn't instruct her on what to say about political issues. Yes, he did teach her how to handle a tamale, because he "didn't want [her] to come down and make the same mistake he did."

She also used the San Antonio visit to break in the new Citizens Band radio her daughter Susan had given her the week before. Adopting the CB handle "First Mama," suggested to her by TV comedian Flip Wilson, she rode around the state in a blue Chrysler making idle chitchat with dumbfounded truckers. "I told them there were a lot of smokies at my front door," she later told reporters, in reference to the police escort her caravan received in San Antonio.

The Ford campaign also got some help in Texas from Jack Ford, the first couple's twenty-four-year-old son. Like all the Ford kids,

Jack had the free-spirited qualities of his mom combined with his dad's knack for self-effacement. The Ford children were the first White House kids who were true products of the rock 'n' roll era, and they had parents who didn't seem particularly mortified that a bit of '60s counterculture residue had rubbed off on their offspring.

In 1974, Jack invited former Beatle George Harrison to the White House, where the checkered-suited Harrison—joined by his touring pals Ravi Shankar and Billy Preston in a ceiling-scraping Afro—exchanged stiff pleasantries with the president. In 1975, Jack danced with Bianca Jagger at the trendy New York disco Le Jardin and spent time hanging out with Andy Warhol. Most memorably, he admitted to an interviewer from the *Portland Oregonian* that he had smoked marijuana and considered it comparable to beer or wine. In response, the president was careful to say he didn't approve of his son's choice, but viewed his honesty as a "very fine trait."

In April 1976, Jack brought his young-rebel bona fides to the college campuses of Texas on his father's behalf. When asked about Reagan's foreign-policy attacks, Jack said, "I have to scratch my head a little bit. . . . [In college], I was defending my father for being too hawkish, and now I find myself defending him on the other end." Of course, the issue that most Texas college students wanted to hear Jack talk about was his highly publicized relationship with a certain illegal herb. One student wanted to know if Jack had inhaled. With an evasive aplomb that Bill Clinton could have learned from, Jack laughed and simply said, "Executive privilege."[43]

As the Fords worked to drum up support in Texas, tawdry reminders of Watergate kept interfering with their message. *All the President's Men*, the film adaptation of Bob Woodward and Carl Bernstein's odyssey to get to the bottom of the scandal, was one of the most popular movies in the country, and its sequel, *The*

Final Days, had just been released and was already breaking sales records at major American bookstores.

Ford's way of handling his Nixon association was to avoid it as much as possible. He was helped by Reagan's disinclination to make Watergate an issue, mindful as he was that every reminder of it damaged the already-tattered Republican brand. When reporters in Houston asked Ford why he always referred to Nixon as his "predecessor," and never by name, Ford acknowledged that the omission was deliberate. "It's my judgment that [Nixon's connection with Watergate and subsequent resignation] was an unfortunate era and the more all of us forget that unfortunate period, the better off we'll be," he said.[44]

For Steve Bartlett, a Goldwater conservative who'd long idolized Reagan, backing Ford caused him mild ambivalence, but no agonizing sleepless nights. "We had an incumbent Republican president, and John Tower was our leader in Texas, so I fell in line," the former Dallas mayor says. "We knew that Gerald Ford was perhaps a bit too moderate for us, but we figured he was our guy, so we'd just be loyal." That kind of ringing endorsement cuts to the heart of the enthusiasm gap that existed between the Ford and Reagan campaigns in Texas. Ford had a top-down operation, with party loyalists taking their marching orders from state GOP leaders. Reagan had a bottom-up coalition, with grassroots activists banging on the door and trying to force the party leadership to let them in.

As much as the primary was a referendum on Ford's presidency, it was also shaping up as a test of John Tower's clout in the state, and a measure of his tortured, mercurial relationship with Texas Republicans.

CHAPTER 9

SENATOR IN EXILE

No matter how many years he spent in politics, John Tower could not remember people's names.

Actually, no one was ever sure if the senator from Texas was incapable of retaining the names of constituents he met, or simply too disinterested to make the effort. Either way, it marked him from the start as a politician whose successes—and they were considerable—would come in spite of a personality that seemed all wrong for a profession that requires you to press the flesh, make cheerful small talk, and try not to unduly antagonize your allies.

If all politicians have contradictory natures, it's a testament to Tower's complexity that his contradictions were more profound and confusing than those of his peers. A diminutive man with a booming baritone voice, Tower's upset special-election win in the 1961 US Senate race made him the first Republican elected statewide in Texas since Reconstruction. He single-handedly carried the torch for the Texas GOP for at least fifteen years and was the Senate's only Southern Republican until Strom Thurmond defected to the GOP in 1964. If he found himself in a lonely position when he entered the Senate, no one could deny that he'd worked hard to build his party. "John Tower was insistent that we start electing Republican legislators," says Lunz, who earned his political stripes working on Tower's 1961 campaign. "And he talked to Strom Thurmond and helped convince him to become a Republican."

Tower should have been universally beloved by Texas Republicans, but he wasn't. Infamous for his volcanic temper and cutting sarcasm, Tower was widely viewed as arrogant and needlessly confrontational. At the same time, he also drew criticism for his unquestioning loyalty to the party establishment. Jimmy Lyon expressed this view on behalf of many conservatives when he told *Texas Monthly* that there was a troubling "exclusivity" to Tower and his friends. "They don't have the ability to identify with the grassroots," Lyon said."[45]

Widely perceived as sullen and withdrawn, he also had a reputation for being a heavy-drinking, sexually voracious party animal. Respected for his intelligence and sharp command of policy matters, he could also seem bored by and indifferent to the happenings on Capitol Hill.

More comfortable with the company of his own thoughts than with a room full of political supporters, he was nonetheless an electrifying public speaker when he chose to be. "John Tower was the most articulate person," Arthur Troilo remembers. "He did question-and-answer periods with the press, with no notes, that were eloquent, to the point, and quotable. He had a brilliant mind."

By the mid-'70s, Tower was the second-ranking Republican on the Senate's Armed Services Committee. A defense hawk and fiscal conservative, he nonetheless found a way to irritate many of his fellow conservatives, often because of his unusual compulsion to go off message and tangle with members of his own base. "Many of the conservative Republicans tolerated Tower, but they didn't particularly like him," says Mark Elam. "He was an arrogant little guy. He liked to booze it up and he liked the women and he was a chain smoker. He came on campus at Texas A&M one time, and he started giving a speech to what was obviously a conservative audience and he just started arguing with people about abortion. [Tower was pro-choice.] I thought to myself, 'This is not too bright.'"

Elam had transferred to Texas A&M after a year at the University of Texas, and he quickly joined the Young Conservatives at A&M in their petition drive against the Panama Canal treaty. After getting ten thousand signatures, Elam and a friend took the petition to Capitol Hill to present to Tower and Lloyd Bentsen. "Tower spent a little time with us, but he wasn't particularly friendly. We asked him if we could get a picture taken with him, next to a statue of Teddy Roosevelt, just down the hallway from his office. His staff refused to allow us to stand up for a picture, and it became quite obvious that they did that because Tower was so short."

Steve Heinrich says much of the intraparty ill will toward Tower was rooted in the fact that he was the only powerful Texas Republican for nearly a full generation, and party members came to resent that kind of power monopoly. Tower himself often seemed uncomfortable with the burdens of his position. "Those who knew him well would say he was more than a little shy," Heinrich says. "He was a little hard to get to know, but one-on-one he could be very personable. He had a great sense of humor, and he was very bright."

When Tower's perverse streak intersected with his sense of loyalty, the political fallout could be serious. At the 1970 state Republican convention, he battled Houston conservatives when they pushed to get a right-to-work plank in the party platform. He did it at the request of George Bush, who was taking on Lloyd Bentsen in that year's Senate race, and didn't want to go out of his way to antagonize union members. Tower succeeded in killing the right-to-work plank, but hard-core conservatives didn't forget.

In a 1977 *Texas Monthly* profile, Tower was described as a legislative tinkerer who didn't initiate ideas but excelled at responding to other people's proposals. As a Texas lobbyist put it, "He's not an offensive running back. He's a linebacker who tries to cause fumbles."[46]

Ernest Angelo recalls that in 1975, Tower visited Midland and asked Angelo who he planned to support in the upcoming presidential race. "When I said Reagan, he told me that that would be the dumbest thing I would ever do politically," Angelo says.

Texas congressman Ron Paul didn't know Tower at the time, but later became friendly with him. He says the senator never failed to show up at any campaign event that Paul asked him to attend. Paul, the only Texas congressman to endorse Reagan in '76, suspects that Tower's support for Ford had more to do with party unity than personal preference. "I think his beliefs were probably closer to Reagan," Paul says. "But events just sort of pushed him into that, and maybe he thought there was no way they could beat an incumbent president."

In a sense, Tower owed his entire political career to the chronic conservative-liberal ideological split within the Texas Democratic Party. The son of an East Texas Methodist minister, Tower grew up, as he would later recall, "a Southern Democrat, like every well-bred Texas lad." In 1938, at the age of thirteen, he passed out handbills for attorney general candidate Ralph Yarborough, who would go on to become the state's preeminent liberal voice. By the early 1950s, however, Tower had come to identify himself as a conservative Republican, and he ran a hopelessly doomed campaign for the state legislature in 1954.

In 1960, as a little-known North Texas political science professor, he secured the GOP nomination for the US Senate and gave Lyndon Johnson a surprisingly tough challenge in the general election. Fortunately for Tower, Johnson also won his other election that night—for vice president of the United States—and was forced to vacate his Senate seat.

An astounding seventy-one candidates lined up for the nonpartisan special election to fill Johnson's seat, including Tower and the obvious front-runner, moderate Fort Worth congressman Jim Wright. With liberal Democrats eschewing Wright and splitting their vote between two outspoken San Antonio progressives— state senator Henry B. Gonzalez and former state legislator Maury Maverick Jr.—Tower was able to avoid what would have been an almost-certain runoff defeat against Wright. Instead, he went head-to-head with Johnson's interim replacement, Braniff Airlines executive William Blakley, a Dallas Dixiecrat with no discernible political skills and no appeal to the Democratic Party's frustrated left wing.

The liberal *Texas Observer* endorsed Tower, essentially arguing that progressives in the state were already losing seats to "pseudo Democrats," and they'd be no worse off losing them to Republicans. With liberals voting for Tower to teach their own party a lesson, he edged out Blakley in one of the state's great political upsets.

Ford and Tower had been friends since they met on Capitol Hill in the early '60s. In 1974, Ford appointed Tower vice chairman of the Rockefeller Commission, a group headed by Vice President Nelson Rockefeller, and assigned with investigating surveillance abuses by the CIA. In return, Tower committed early, and with great enthusiasm, to Ford's 1976 presidential campaign. The two men were inseparable for much of April 1976, and Tower put his reputation on the line to a degree that he never had before. It was a risky move for a Republican senator in a Democratic state, with a sure-to-be-tough reelection campaign only two years away. In 1977, *Texas Monthly* offered the consensus view on Tower's bet-the-house gamble: "Foolhardy seems the word for Tower's decision to identify so closely with Ford that he turned the Texas primary into a vote of no-confidence in himself."[47]

On April 7, two days after Reagan launched his first Texas campaign swing, Tower got the spin-control game going by telling reporters that a mere victory in Texas couldn't save Reagan's campaign—he needed at least 75 percent of the vote. "Unless Reagan sweeps the Texas primary, the general assumption is that his candidacy is through," Tower said. "Should he even do as well as break even with Ford in Texas, that's not enough. Then you have to think about the aggregate delegate vote."[48]

The aggregate delegate vote overwhelmingly favored Ford. Going into Texas, the president had sewn up 268 delegates (nearly one-fourth of the 1,130 he needed for the nomination) to 137 for Reagan, and he had an informal lock on the bulk of New York's 154 and Pennsylvania's 103 delegates. Even Reagan's most ardent partisans knew that the numbers were conspiring against him.

Tower's support for Ford worried Reagan staffers, who thought it might squeeze the life out of their candidate's campaign. "It was distressing, because John Tower had a letter-perfect conservative voting record and he wasn't just mildly for Ford, he was very strongly for Ford," Jeff Bell says. "He probably said some things about Reagan that he wished to his dying day that he hadn't said. But he basically had the view that Reagan wasn't qualified to be president. It seemed like, 'God, if we can't get John Tower in Texas, who are we going to get?'"

Tower tried to downplay Reagan's obvious signs of strength in Texas by contending that the Gipper's followers were not as numerous as their decibel count suggested. "There's no question that Reagan has a lot of support in Texas and it's very vocal, but I think you get a distorted impression of how strong it is by virtue of the fact that the Reagan people are far more vocal than the Ford people are," he said."[49]

At a Four-for-Ford rally in the San Antonio suburb of Boerne on April 22, Tower made his most stinging attacks yet on Reagan's credentials. "Based on the somewhat simplistic sloganeering I've heard so far in his campaign, I doubt seriously Governor Reagan has the experience or grasp of national issues to handle the presidency near as well as Ford," Tower said.

Statements like this made Tower—a man who'd actively worked in 1964 to secure the GOP presidential nomination for conservative godfather Barry Goldwater—dartboard material for right-wing Reaganites. For much of his time in Washington, he'd been the outcast, the man viewed with a polite wariness by Democrats who ruled the state's congressional delegation. Now, he found himself on the verge of being exiled to the margins of the Texas political party he'd done so much to build.

It never occurred to the leaders of the Ford campaign that Tower was taking a political beating for his close association with the president. As far as they were concerned, they had the most powerful Texas Republican on their side, and that had to translate into votes. "John Tower really represented the entire south for Republicans at that time," Jim Lunz says. "That's why Ford felt like he was going to carry Texas. The [party] loyalists were sticking with the incumbent, and John Tower took that role."

The support of Republican insiders did Tower (or Ford) little good when the crusading Reagan 76ers crashed the party with a vengeance. For much of the next two years, Tower served his political penance: The Reaganites denied him a seat at the '76 national convention and threatened to put a more ideologically pure conservative up against him in the 1978 senatorial primary. Nonetheless, Tower fought off a tough challenge in '78 from Democratic congressman Bob Krueger, an urbane, Oxford-educated literature professor whom Tower mockingly called "Little Lord Fauntleroy." Even by Texas standards, it was a mean, nasty mud-wrestling match. A Krueger campaign operative wrote and circulated to Texas newspapers an op-ed that brought up persistent old rumors about Tower's penchant for drinking and womanizing. Tower had a fuse whose length always seemed to be directly proportional to his own diminutive stature, and the op-ed enraged him so much that he pointedly refused to shake Krueger's hand at a candidate forum.

By 1983, when Tower announced that he would not seek another term in the Senate, he had settled into a position as wise party elder, appreciated by his fellow Republicans for his seminal role in breaking the Democratic monopoly in the state. The old resentments weren't forgotten, but they were put in the context of a long political career that had begun with him as an electoral fluke and Capitol Hill outsider and ended with him a respected member of a party in ascendance.

In 1986, Reagan named him to head a commission to study the Iran-Contra scandal and determine what National Security Council mistakes had been made. The commission's report criticized the actions of several administration figures but concluded—in the face of contradictory testimony—that Reagan himself did not know about the covert arms-for-hostages deal with Iran or the diversion of funds from that sale to the Contra rebels in Nicaragua.

If Tower thought he had successfully recast himself as a post-partisan public servant, however, he was wrong. In 1989, President George H. W. Bush nominated him for defense secretary, a job he'd long coveted. But Tower's old Senate colleagues refused to confirm his nomination, largely because of newly revived rumors of his reckless personal behavior and concerns about his close ties as a consultant with defense contractors. Once again, those who knew him best had rejected him. Two years later, on April 5, 1991, he died in a plane crash near Brunswick, Georgia. Karl Rove, the Texas consultant who had already propelled Rick Perry to state-wide office and would later guide George W. Bush to the White House, offered as an epitaph the simple salute that Tower often felt he was denied in life: "[He] helped create the modern Republican Party in Texas."

Even Tower's harshest Republican critics would grant him that.

CHAPTER 10

★ RON PAUL'S GOLD STANDARD

Ron Paul has only been to one Republican National Convention in his life, and it wasn't the year he ran for the party's presidential nomination. Go figure.

Paul was shut out of the 2008 RNC, despite his impressive fundraising money bombs and respectable showing in a string of early presidential primaries, partly because his blunt criticism of the Iraq War gave the Republican National Committee a pounding headache and, more significantly, because he refused to endorse party standard-bearer John McCain. "They took my credentials away," he says, "because I wasn't enthusiastic enough about our nominee."

The one time Paul made it to the RNC was not to celebrate his own presidential campaign but to cast his vote as part of the hundred-member Texas delegation for Ronald Reagan. Paul had been picked as an at-large delegate at the 1976 Republican State Convention in June, largely because he was the highest-ranking GOP officeholder in Texas who had endorsed Reagan in his battle against Ford. The fact that he was the biggest name the Reagan forces had at their disposal says more about what an outsider campaign they were running than it does about Paul's prominence at that time.

Paul hardly qualified as a big wheel in the Texas GOP when he endorsed Reagan in April 1976. A Lake Jackson obstetrician and gynecologist who had served as a flight surgeon for the US Air Force and the US Air National Guard in the 1960s, Paul was elected to Congress exactly four weeks before the Texas presidential primary. He didn't even take the congressional oath of office until three days after Reagan began his first campaign swing in Texas.

Unlike most of his fellow members of Congress, Paul had shown no previous interest in party politics. The son of a Pittsburgh dairy owner, he studied at Duke University School of Medicine, where he spent his idle time kicking back with various tomes on the intricacies of free-market economics. After finishing medical school, he and his wife Carol moved to Detroit to serve his internship and a one-year internal medicine residency.

During the Cuban Missile Crisis, he was drafted by the US military and stationed in San Antonio. In 1968, at the age of thirty-three, he set up his medical practice near the Gulf Coast of East Texas, where he delivered so many babies (an estimated four thousand) that the running joke about his political career became that people in Lake Jackson voted for him largely because he'd helped bring one of their family members into the world.

Over the years, Paul has emerged as an equal-opportunity exasperator. Conservatives love his strict libertarian rejection of federal social programs, which has earned him the Capitol Hill nickname of "Dr. No." On the other hand, his strict libertarian rejection of expensive defense programs—and his outspoken disdain for the nation's history of military intervention around the world—aggravates neo-cons, who dismiss him as a deluded crank who doesn't understand the "war on terror." His insistence that hard drugs—including heroin—should be legalized so outraged the late chain-smoking shock-talk television host Morton Downey Jr. that Downey once threatened to "puke on" Paul.

Liberals who applauded his bold criticism of the Iraq War in the 2008 GOP presidential debates, however, must cope with his contention that the federal government went too far with the 1964 Civil Rights Act (he doesn't believe the United States should dictate business practices to private entities), his support for the elimination of both the federal income tax and federal funding for education, and his willingness to associate with right-wing extremists and conspiracy theorists (including 9/11 Truthers).

Nonetheless, Paul was something of a revelation in the 2008 presidential race. When he appeared on Bill Maher's HBO talk show, *Real Time*, the reaction was staggering. Maher's reliably liberal studio audience—which only moments earlier had been nonplussed by the presence of actor Ben Affleck—screamed for Paul like tweens with front-row tickets at a Justin Bieber concert and spent much of the show's final half-hour chanting "Paul! Paul! Paul!" Maher could barely believe what he was hearing. This, he told Paul, was the warmest greeting that any Republican had ever received on his show.

While Paul persuasively argued that he was the most conservative candidate in the 2008 GOP field, he attracted some progressives and moderates because they perceived him not as an ideologue but as a truth-teller who refused to be chained to any party's set of assumptions.

In fact, Paul might be less interested in the mechanics of party politics than any major-party presidential candidate of the modern era. Going into the 2012 campaign, he had no memory of ever meeting Rick Perry, the preeminent figure in Texas Republican politics over the last decade, and he seems to take little satisfaction in the fact that his state his shifted from blue to red over the course of his political career. He comes across as remarkably oblivious to partisan considerations, quick to light up when the conversation moves to economic and fiscal theories, and equally quick to lose interest when the topic shifts to the nuts and bolts of electioneering. In that sense, Paul has remained a model of consistency over the last thirty-five years. While his foreign-policy perspective has changed (from a fairly conventional Cold Warrior to a near-isolationist), his loyalty has always been to ideas, rather than a party affiliation.

As a young doctor, Paul didn't think of himself as a member of any party and took more inspiration from the market-libertarian philosophy behind Friedrich Hayek's *The Road to Serfdom* than the campaign rhetoric of any political candidate. Developing into something of a free-market, armchair economist, Paul believed Richard Nixon made a colossal mistake in 1971 by moving the American monetary system away from the gold standard, making the dollar a free-floating currency that can be printed with impunity by the Federal Reserve.

Deeply bothered by Nixon's decision, Paul decided to run for Congress in 1974 and was surprised when he received the eager backing of a hard-up, scandal-plagued Republican Party. "I had never gone to a precinct meeting, never ran for anything, didn't know anybody in the party," he says. "But nobody cared who I was in 1974, because that was a Watergate year. That year, nobody wanted to run, and there were no Republicans in Texas. I was thinking of running as an independent, but when I talked to the Republican Party, they said, 'Yeah, yeah, come around,' and they encouraged me to do it."

Paul lost the general election to Democratic incumbent Robert Casey, but when Casey resigned in early 1976 to accept Gerald Ford's offer to head the Federal Maritime Commission, Paul decided to give it a second try. "The Republican Party was very supportive," Paul says. "They didn't know exactly who I was or what I was up to, but they said, 'You already ran, you've got some name recognition. Run again!'"

On April 3, 1976, Paul won a stunning victory, defeating veteran Democrat Bob Gammage by nearly 10 percent in a special-election runoff. Almost immediately, he endorsed Reagan in the presidential primary, making him the only one of the state's four Republican US representatives to oppose Ford. "I had not met Reagan at the time, though I met him quite a few times after that," Paul says. "I first got interested in him when he gave that speech for Goldwater in '64. So I knew he was more down my way of thinking than Ford would have ever been."

Paul says his basic political philosophy was established by the time he heard Reagan's 1964 speech, but adds that it gradually grew stricter and more defined. "As the years went on, I became more libertarian, and although Reagan respected the libertarians—he said once that libertarianism was the basis of all conservatism—in 1964 I had not worked some of these things out and I probably had a much different attitude about foreign policy," Paul says. "As the years went by, I became much more of a noninterventionist and much more concerned about civil liberties."

For Paul, libertarianism is an absolute, a fixed ideal, and he generally refuses to give an inch on policy issues. He sees that as incrementalism, the enemy of all libertarian purists. As a result, Paul voted in 2000 against a Congressional Medal to honor Ronald and Nancy Reagan, simply because the cost of minting the gold was $30,000, and Paul doesn't believe the US Constitution gives Congress the authority to spend taxpayer money on awards. Because he doesn't believe in government-funded health care, Paul has refused to accept Medicaid or Medicare payments from his patients, opting instead to work out a payment plan with them or perform the medical service for free.

As a forty-year-old freshman congressman, Paul bore a vague physical resemblance to the young George H. W. Bush: wiry, athletic (Bush played baseball at Yale while Paul was a Pennsylvania high school track star), narrow-jawed, with grackle-black hair arranged in a neat preppy cut, and possessing a halting smile that camouflaged a steely confidence. Once they opened their mouths, however, these two Texas Republicans were not easily confused with each other. Bush was a team player: a compromiser, a facilitator who felt most comfortable traveling down the middle of the road but would periodically steer to the left or right if it got him where he wanted to go. Paul viewed the Republican Party the way an iconoclastic punk rocker views his record label: They might provide a brand name and a distribution system to get his message out, but that doesn't mean they can tamper with the content of that message.

Three months after taking office, Paul told the members of the Dallas County Republican Men's Club that they needed to stop diluting their message, contending that both conservatives and liberals had "drifted into a pragmatic approach" designed to paper over their differences. "Very few politicians go into office with a philosophy," Paul said. From the beginning, Paul knew that, if nothing else, he was a member of that select club.[50]

He also felt confident that Reagan, unlike Ford, possessed a clear vision of how government should run. Although Paul and Reagan didn't meet until well after the '76 primary campaign, the association helped both men. The energy of the Reagan movement helped Paul galvanize conservatives in his East Texas counties, while Paul's endorsement of Reagan after the April 3 congressional election helped counteract the prevailing narrative established by party leaders: Ford was their standard-bearer, Reagan supporters were being disloyal, and all the division was hurting the party's chances in November. "Representative Paul was one of only four congressmen in the entire nation who came out and endorsed

Reagan over Ford," says Mark Elam, who worked on both men's campaigns that year and later became Paul's campaign manager. "He was active in the leadership of that campaign."

Paul's special-election win didn't afford him much time to build a record in Congress. That November, only seven months after taking office, he would face the voters again, in a general election. At his first news conference as a congressman, Paul talked about his desire to slash the size of government but also hinted that this goal would be impossible without major changes in Washington. When asked what kind of record he'd be able to present to voters in November, he said, "I think it will be a slim record. I'm realistic."

In November 1976, Paul lost the congressional seat he'd settled into only seven months before when Gammage took their return match by only 268 votes (slightly more than one-tenth of 1 percent of the total vote). It was an election marked by confusion and human error, as Houston Election Central mistakenly fed the state election bureau district-wide figures instead of simply the numbers for Harris County. As a result, Paul woke up the morning after the election thinking he'd won by ten thousand votes only to find that he'd come up short.

Two years later, with campaign help from Reagan, Paul won back his seat from Gammage. In his first full term in Congress, he began to develop a reputation for drafting eccentric legislation that his supporters saw as brilliantly symbolic and his detractors branded as lame-brained.

Blaming the federal government for runaway inflation, in 1979 he introduced a bill that would give the members of Congress a pay cut every time the cost of living went up. The salary cuts would be in direct proportion to increases in the Consumer Price Index. "This is the quickest way I know to educate Congressmen in the realities of economics," Paul told reporters. "Congress' big spending and its deficit spending—combined with political attempts to stimulate the economy for election reasons—causes immense harm to the poor, the aged, and the middle class."[51] To the surprise of no one, the bill went nowhere.

That same year, he submitted legislation requiring members of Congress to receive their colleagues' approval (by a three-fourths vote) for any overseas trip they intended to take at taxpayer expense. He also tweaked hypocrisy wherever he perceived it to be, sending out a mailer with a picture of his humble Chevette parked next to Democratic House Speaker Tip O'Neill's chauffeur-driven limousine, with a caption bashing politicians for using gas guzzlers.

In 1980, he outraged Democrats and Republicans alike when he complained that $50 million in US aid for an earthquake-ravaged Italy might be "stolen or wasted" by a corrupt Italian bureaucracy. Rep. Silvio Conte, an Italian American Republican from Massachusetts, challenged Paul to be "man enough" to apologize to the people of Italy.

Between embarrassing his Capitol Hill colleagues and baffling business leaders back home in Texas with his refusal to support pork-barrel spending programs targeted for his district, Paul became a marked man. He hadn't even finished his first full term when a Dump Paul movement started gaining traction in his district. But neither Democratic-driven redistricting efforts nor Republican establishment plans to find a viable opponent for him could ever knock him out of his seat.

Also, by 1981 he had a clear ally in the White House—a man who respected Paul's quirks, even when he didn't share them. "I remember having a personal flight with Reagan on the presidential helicopter," Paul says.

We both needed to go to Houston, and we were both flying together. We talked about the gold standard. He was sympathetic to my points. We had a good thirty-minute visit, which is pretty unusual for a young congressman to spend that much time with a president. He was very likeable. At one point in the early '80s, he needed a vote on the B-1 bomber. I had made public announcements that the B-1 was too old-fashioned and we didn't need it. He personally called me and asked me if I could vote for that. I told him that after stating a public position it would be real hard to go back on my word. He said, "Oh, okay, I understand." Very, very polite, he didn't do any arm-twisting. I got to thinking, "If that had been LBJ, he would have sent an army over here."

Despite his personal fondness for Reagan and their shared set of principles, Paul eventually grew deeply dissatisfied with the Reagan administration. The Gipper had made deficit reduction a central plank of his bid for the White House, but by the end of his first year in office, a combination of tax cuts, military-spending increases, and a crippling national recession had caused the federal deficit to explode. By the end of 1981, David Stockman, Reagan's young budget wizard, went public with his frustration over the administration's inability to get a handle on its own spending numbers. "At the beginning, I was excited about what I thought was going to happen," Paul says. "But I voted against the first Reagan budget, which passed in a Democratic House. I thought it was horrible. The year before, Carter had a deficit of $38 billion, and the proposal for this one was a $45 billion deficit. I thought, 'Why are we voting for this? Every Republican voted against the Carter budget, and this is worse.' Then that deficit turned out to be triple what they'd proposed. By that time, I figured, 'There's not going to be any revolution.' Spending exploded, deficits exploded, they kept printing the money, and kept building these huge financial bubbles that look like they're coming to an end."

Paul became so disenchanted with eight years of Reaganomics that in 1988, at the end of Reagan's second term, he bolted from the GOP and ran for president as a libertarian. It proved to be a test drive of sorts for his 2008 presidential campaign, when he essentially ran as an independent under the GOP umbrella.

Even Reagan, whose brand of conservatism tasted like it was 200-proof in 1976, had the pragmatist's self-preservation instinct to dilute it when he actually had to govern. He'd shown that even as governor of California. Paul doesn't think that way, which is both his greatest political strength and weakness. For a few weeks in 1976, however, Paul and Reagan, two true believers seemingly straddling the political fringe, gave each other a small boost at a moment when both of their political careers needed any bit of credibility they could get.

CHAPTER 11
STRETCH DRIVE

In the fall of 1975, a San Antonio Republican leader named Van Archer had a private meeting in Washington, DC, with Reagan communications director Lyn Nofziger. At that point, Reagan had not yet officially committed to challenging Ford, and Archer—a dedicated conservative Republican from the Goldwater school— thought he'd offer Nofziger a few words of encouragement. Archer told him, "If Reagan runs, we will win every [district] race in Texas."

Nofziger didn't say much in response, and Archer was convinced that Nofziger didn't believe him. An hour later, after they'd finished talking, Archer found himself in a crowded elevator, unaware that Nofziger was standing in the back. "This woman started asking me about Texas," Archer recalls. "I told her, 'If Reagan runs, we'll win 80 percent of the delegates in Texas.' Well, Nofziger heard that and he blurted out, from the back of the elevator, 'You said you were going to win 100 percent of them!'"

Such were the pitfalls of the expectations game in the Reagan-Ford race. Both candidates positioned themselves as underdogs in Texas, and both had valid reasons—beyond their obvious desires to lower media expectations as much as possible. Ford had the establishment, Reagan had grassroots passion; Ford had national momentum, Reagan had regional appeal. In truth, nobody knew where the two candidates stood with Texas voters, but going into the final week before the primary, all the political constellations seemed to be aligning for Ford, and he could barely contain his optimism.

Eight days before the primary, a *New York Times*/CBS News poll found that Ford was viewed more favorably than any other candidate in the race, including all Democrats. The poll found that Republicans across the country favored Ford over Reagan by a three-to-two margin, and even when Reagan touched on a vulnerable issue for Ford, he had been unable to sway voters. For example, 64 percent of Republicans opposed Ford's policy of détente with the Soviet Union, but only 40 percent of those détente-haters preferred Reagan over the president. It also found that Ford's always-precarious standing as a strong leader had inched its way up from 54 to 59 percent.

On April 28, a Harris Poll showed Ford with an even more commanding national lead over Reagan among Republican voters. Harris found that Republicans favored Ford by nearly two to one, and even on the contentious, hot-button security issue of dealing with the Soviet Union, Ford was preferred by 57 percent to only 23 percent for Reagan. "Even Reagan's most ardent backers admit that Ford's chances of winning the White House for the GOP in November are better than their own candidate's," Harris concluded.[52]

Meanwhile, Ford's national delegate lead over Reagan was growing close to prohibitive, and the large crowds he generated at his Texas stops convinced him that the momentum was flowing his way. Ford had only made one swing into Texas going into the final week of the campaign, allowing surrogates such as John Tower to get his message out for him. But on Tuesday, April 27, he began a concentrated four-day blitz meant to close the deal with Texas Republicans.

While Ford had been on the defensive during his first round of Texas campaign appearances, he took a more aggressive stance this time. At Tyler Junior College, he accused Reagan of making "simplistic and superficial" charges about the nation's military strength. Rather than simply defending his record as commander-in-chief, or calling Reagan reckless, Ford ridiculed the specifics of Reagan's attacks. Noting that one of Reagan's "favorite charges" was that the Soviet Union had twice as many people in the military as the United States, he challenged Reagan on the best way to close that gap.

Ford argued that the only way the United States could double its forces from 2 million to 4 million, as Reagan wanted, would be by reinstituting the draft and pulling billions of dollars out of weapons programs to meet the manpower costs. "No reputable military expert I know has suggested such a course of action, which would undermine rather than strengthen our defenses," Ford said.[53]

For the first time in weeks, Ford also tried to force Reagan off his Panama Canal and Kissinger sound bites and into a defensive posture on domestic issues. Ford's campaign sent Texas voters a mailer reminding them about Reagan's infamous $90 billion plan to cut federal spending by shifting budgetary responsibilities to the states. The extra burden on states recommended by Reagan, the mailer said, would force Texas to adopt a state income tax. Given that Texans prided themselves on avoiding the kind of tax burdens imposed by large Northeastern states, a Texas state income tax was a payment whose best chance of collection would come by prying it from the cold dead hands of its residents.

Hours before arriving in Tyler, Ford made a Louisiana stop with one eye firmly focused on Texas voters. Dropping into Bossier City—a town in the northwest corner of Louisiana, where the Bayou State meets the Texas and Arkansas borders—for the annual

"Holiday in Dixie" spring festival, Ford took advantage of the fact that the event was televised live in East Texas. He even courted the conservative Democratic bloc that Reagan had been wooing for weeks, appearing at the festival with two Democrats: Louisiana governor Edwin Edwards and Congressman Joe Waggoner. Ford praised Waggoner as "invaluable to [him] . . . in the Congress as well as in the White House." Waggoner returned the favor by calling Ford the "hope of the free world."[54]

Even before his Texas tour, Ford tried to shore up his support on the right with two well-orchestrated—if largely symbolic—policy announcements. On Monday, April 26, he asked Congress for an additional $322 million in funding to continue production of the Minuteman missile, a request for which Reagan gladly took credit. The following day, Ford tried to shore up his tough-on-crime credentials by calling for stricter drug laws, including minimum mandatory sentences for traffickers, who he called "merchants of death." Ford acknowledged that the nation was losing the so-called war on drugs and called it "a national tragedy."

Emboldened by the large crowds that greeted him in East Texas, Ford grew so confident that he veered off message and boldly predicted a victory in the May 1 primary. Later, realizing that he'd violated a central tenet of the political-expectations game, he tried to walk his statement back by saying he wouldn't make a prediction.

Nonetheless, the signs looked promising. For one thing, Ford—so often the target of political barbs—was starting to get under Reagan's skin. In a speech before thirty-five hundred supporters at the Houston Music Theater, Reagan sounded genuinely miffed over Ford's recent criticisms of him. "I am trying to hold my temper despite some of the campaign tactics I have seen in the last few days," Reagan said, shuffling the four-by-six index cards that formed the basis of almost every campaign speech he gave. Reagan said that the "simplistic and superficial charges" Ford had accused him of were actually "facts and figures from Ford's own top military advisers" on the issue of Soviet superiority. "But I would not like to get intemperate as Mr. Ford has been in the last few days," Reagan said. "I don't want it to seem it is catching in Texas."[55]

In the first hint of a budding duel with Betty Ford that would turn surreal at that summer's Republican National Convention, Nancy Reagan arrived in San Antonio just as the First Lady—and her CB radio—was departing. Nancy told the press she didn't consider it appropriate to advise her husband on political matters, a statement that sounded like a subtle swipe at the unabashedly opinioned Betty Ford. When asked about the Equal Rights Amendment, one of Betty's pet causes, Nancy responded: "I am for equal rights. But I don't think the best way to go about it is the amendment. I think there are certain protections given women in the Constitution that the amendment would take away."[56]

On April 22, both women spent the day campaigning in Austin. Betty Ford took a tour of the LBJ Library with Lady Bird Johnson, while eight members of the Austin Right to Life Committee stood outside waving signs as a protest against the First Lady's pro-choice stance. When a reporter asked her to name one thing she'd like to see her husband add to his presidential checklist, she shot back, "Appoint a woman to the Supreme Court."

That same day, Nancy Reagan took twenty Austin campaign workers out for a seafood quiche lunch and held a news conference in which she said she would never lobby her husband to appoint women to high positions. She identified her pet national cause as the Foster Grandparent program ("I think we tend to forget about the elderly") and brushed off any suggestion that she, like Betty Ford, would be willing to call herself "First Mama."[57]

While Betty Ford freely courted controversy with her political candor, Nancy Reagan scrupulously avoided any public utterances that clashed even slightly with those from her husband. For all her efforts to remain innocuous, however, Nancy was a polarizing figure among Reagan's Texas diehards.

One North Texas campaign staffer frequently required to accompany Nancy to campaign fundraisers has nothing but bad memories of the experience. "I didn't really care for her," the former staffer says. "When she would come in, she would always come in with her retinue: her hairdresser, her personal secretary, her bodyguard. She was just a spoiled brat."

Ernest Angelo saw another side of Nancy Reagan during one of her campaign visits to Houston:

> It was almost midnight and my wife and I met her at the airport. From there, I took her to her hotel room. She had a reputation of being kind of cold and stiff, so I'm trying to do my best because it's late at night and she's tired. We go up to the room, I open the door, and a guy sits up in bed. So the room was already occupied. I'm thinking, "I'm dead, she's gonna kill me!" But she died laughing. She was not upset at all.

Aware that electability had become one of Ford's chief campaign hooks, Reagan's backers tried to chip away at the president's argument in the final days before the primary. Their fundamental point boiled down to this: Forget what the polls are telling you. Ford is a Washington insider, and no Washington insider is going to win the presidential election this year.

On Tuesday, April 27, John Sears held a press conference in San Antonio and pointed out that Ford had never before run for office on a national or statewide level. It raised questions, Sears said, whether Ford could mount an effective national campaign. Sears also suggested that Ford was out of step with the national mood, noting that Jimmy Carter was winning primaries on an anti-Washington theme, and Ford—unlike Reagan—wouldn't have a good answer for this outsider message.

The following day, ACU chairman M. Stanton Evans visited San Antonio and said Ford would be a "sitting duck" in a general-election campaign against Carter. Evans described Ford as a man who talked like a conservative on the campaign trail but didn't govern like one. "Reagan represents an effort to change the momentum, to start subtracting and put a little more money in our pockets and less for the bureaucrats and social engineers," Evans said.[58]

While Ford was drawing large crowds everywhere he went, a worrisome pattern had emerged. In Lubbock, fourteen thousand people turned up to see him speak at the Municipal Coliseum, but nearly half of them walked out while he was taking questions from the audience. The same thing happened in Houston and Spring Branch. People came because they wanted to see an American president in person, but once they'd achieved that, many of them seemed to lose interest in what Ford had to say.

Reagan audiences, by contrast, tended to be smaller, but they inevitably left the building more stirred up than when they entered. "Reagan's visit to Midland was huge," Angelo recalls. "It was held at one of the high schools and we had to end up with TV sets on the outside for people, because we had way more than the seven hundred people that could get in the auditorium."

On Thursday, April 29, two days before the Texas primary, Reagan caught a break when Hubert Humphrey, the last major hope of Democratic insiders eager to stop Jimmy Carter's methodical march to the nomination, tearfully announced that he would not enter the race. Any Texas Democrats hoping to cast an anybody-but-Carter vote in the primary had to recognize that Carter was now an inevitability. With the Democratic race over but for the shouting (and even the shouting would be minimal in '76 for this historically fractious party), more Texas eyes turned to the highly competitive, high-stakes race on the Republican side.

The day before the Texas primary, Reagan made a noontime visit to the Alamo and brought some Hollywood reinforcements with him: old friend Jimmy Stewart, veteran character actor Lloyd Nolan, singing cowboy Rex Allen, former Miss America Mary Ann Mobley, and her actor husband Gary Collins. The music was provided by San Antonio Dixieland group Happy Jazz. Decked out in a crisp gray suit with a white cowboy hat, a beaming Reagan plunged into the middle of a wildly excited crowd that treated him more like a returning war hero than a pol shilling for votes in the eleventh hour of his wobbly candidacy. Reagan's estimated crowd of five thousand was less than one-third of what Ford had attracted three weeks earlier, but its enthusiasm was on a completely different scale.

Pulling together all the themes that had marked his decade-plus in politics, Reagan recited a litany that read like Goldwater 101 (but sounded like Goldwater 101 as delivered by an expert Hollywood pitch man): The federal government is taking forty-four cents of every dollar Americans earn; public employees should not have the right to strike; gun control is an affront to personal liberty; big government makes people small; welfare is "destroying people instead of salvaging them"; federal aid to education has become federal interference in education. When Reagan punctuated his series of attacks by asking the crowd whether they agreed with Ford that the federal government should keep on functioning as it is, the response was a thunderous "No!"

At every stop on his final campaign day, he implored Democrats to join his cause. Going into Texas, the assumption was that big turnouts were good for Ford and bad for Reagan. The reasoning was that Reagan's appeal was narrower, and as more Republicans showed up to vote, Reagan's small, hard-core following diminished in importance. In every primary where the turnout had been strong, Ford had won. In North Carolina, the one state Reagan had taken, turnout had been poor.

In Texas, however, Reagan was preparing to turn all those assumptions upside down. His team prayed for a big turnout and sensed that victory hinged on Democratic defections. "I don't just say, 'my fellow Republicans, I need your vote.' I address myself to Democrats and independents as well," Reagan said in Dallas. "[Ford has said] I don't have a broad enough base of support to win a national election. But I say I won the governor's race in California where Democrats outnumber Republicans two-to-one."[59] Meanwhile, Reagan workers handed out flyers that said, "Democrats: you will *not* be committing a major indiscretion if you vote this year, in the Republican primary."

The night before the primary, millions of Americans tuned in to ABC to watch heavyweight champion Muhammad Ali win a lackluster fifteen-round decision over challenger Jimmy Young. (Ali had by this point declared his admiration for Jimmy Carter, citing his "good looks, the way he talks," and his farming background.)

At Reagan's Houston headquarters, there was nervousness. From the start, Barnhart believed that Reagan needed to win at least sixty-six of the state's one hundred delegates to have a decent shot at the nomination. Now, even a close win seemed questionable. "The mood was apprehensive," Steve Munisteri says. "We thought it would be so close that on election day, when we got a call from an elderly voter, they asked me to go pick her up and take her to the polls, because it could be so tight that every vote would count. Nobody had Reagan ahead by a dramatic margin."

The day before the election, *New York Times* reporter James

Sterba suggested that Reagan had peaked too early in Texas and Ford had put himself in position to pull off a nomination-sealing win: "Political leaders here believe that last-minute campaigning by President Ford has cut substantially into Ronald Reagan's early lead in Texas, turning tomorrow's presidential primary into a cliffhanger that they said was too close to call."[60]

Ford didn't need a victory in Texas. He simply needed a close outcome to maintain his huge delegate lead and prevent Reagan from building serious momentum. A narrow loss for Ford would leave his unofficial advantage (counting his big projected haul from New York) at about three hundred delegates, with Reagan's home state of California the only realistic possibility for Reagan to make major cuts into that lead. Anything short of a big win in Texas would render the Reagan effort a dead campaign walking.

Even with the media suggesting that Ford was gaining strength, his forces on the ground weren't so sure. "We were very worried about the primary," Arthur Troilo remembers. "We never thought that we were very much ahead. We thought we were pretty even. But as it went on, Reagan was gaining strength. In the end, it showed." Steve Heinrich, who worked with Troilo out of Ford's San Antonio headquarters, says, "I felt that we weren't going to win. You could feel the energy and the grassroots with Reagan."

Even the most optimistic turnout predictions from GOP leaders had topped out at 300,000, but by the middle of the day on Saturday, it was clear that the actual numbers would be much higher. There were long lines in Dallas, Houston, Lubbock, and McAllen. In rural areas, many voting sites didn't have enough paper ballots to meet the unprecedented demand. The Republican Party was undermanned and overwhelmed. "We had some feel that it was coming, but we didn't have the tools to deal with it," Jim Lunz says. "We didn't have any way of equipping ourselves with the volunteers who would commit the fourteen-hour day, and then some, because they had to count those paper ballots in quadruplicate, and write out all those forms and bring it all into the election center. Some people spent all night doing that paperwork after the election was over."

State senator Kent Hance watched many of his fellow Democrats defect because of their fascination with the GOP presidential race. "With the Democratic primary, everybody presumed Carter was going to get it, so there wasn't any big push for anybody there," Hance says. "So a lot of my friends, and people that were conservative Democrats, they went over and voted for Reagan, 'cause they liked him."

Van Archer, whose name appeared on the ballot as a Reagan delegate in South Texas, remembers feeling supremely confident on election day. "I kind of knew we were going to win," he says. "Every part of [San Antonio] I called, they'd say, 'Damn right, I'm for Ronald Reagan.'"

While Jimmy Lyon spent much of the day throwing up at the Houston headquarters, Angelo and Barnhart tried to calm his nerves by assuring him that Reagan was going to win big. Angelo's confidence was not merely based on political intuition. He had spies giving him inside information that could generously be described as a secret form of exit polling. "I had people around the state in the key counties who were involved with counting the primary absentee votes," Angelo says.

> They were counting them before the polls closed, which was legitimate, but it probably wasn't legitimate for them to tell me what the results were. But that's what they did. I wasn't sharing it with anyone except our own people, but I knew by three o'clock in the afternoon that we were going to clean their clock. In key places, we were winning, not just by a majority, but by a huge majority. So we were telling Jimmy, "Don't sweat it, we know we've got this thing locked up."

Nancy Reagan was nearly as worried as Lyon. That afternoon, she called Angelo for an update. "I said, 'We're going to get 100 percent [of the delegates],' Angelo says. "She said, 'Oh Ernie, don't say that. Don't get carried away.' I didn't tell her why I knew, but I said, 'We're going to win 'em all. Don't worry.'"

Ray Hutchison remembers accompanying Reagan to Love Field in Dallas that afternoon as Reagan prepared to leave Texas for a campaign swing in Indiana. Reagan asked him what kind of results he foresaw in the Texas primary, and Hutchison responded that he expected Reagan to win overwhelmingly. Reagan looked surprised and asked Hutchison if he would call him in Indiana that night with news of the results.

As the numbers started pouring in, they confirmed what the heavy turnout seemed to suggest: Reagan was handing Ford the most brutal shellacking any sitting president had ever suffered in an intraparty contest. "It was unbelievable," Bell says of the victory party that night in Houston. "It was pretty clear not long after the polls closed that we might actually win ninety-six out of ninety-six delegates. I'm sure that a lot of people were getting drunk. It was overwhelming. Primaries were much more spaced out at that time, and this was only the second win for Reagan. We knew that winning ninety-six out of ninety-six delegates in a state where Ford had the entire establishment could have a big impact on the subsequent primaries."

Reagan received 66 percent of the vote (278,300) to only 33 percent for Ford (139,944) and swept all twenty-four of the state's congressional districts. Reagan called in from Indiana that night and sang "The Eyes of Texas" over the phone to his campaign revelers in Houston. Instantly, the GOP race had gone from being a veritable lock for Ford to anybody's ballgame, and the Ford team could hardly believe it. The *New York Times* accurately termed Ford's loss "devastating." All hope for an early knockout was gone. Ford's people now knew they'd be battling Reagan until the convention.

That night, the president and First Lady attended the annual White House Correspondents Dinner at the Washington Hilton Hotel, already aware that the news looked bad from Texas. They managed to grin their way through an interminable night that included meet-and-greets and a performance by Tennessee Ernie Ford and Opryland USA. John Tower and Peter Kaye blamed the Democratic crossover vote for Ford's poor performance. Tower invited further derision from Reagan acolytes by implying that the challenger would pay a political price down the line for his heated rhetoric: "The unanswered question is whether this victory gives Governor Reagan viable momentum or whether national perception of him as a result of this campaign makes his victory a Pyrrhic one." A President Ford Committee spokesman told the *Houston Chronicle* that Ford "did everything he could do," but he couldn't compete with Reagan's "rabid constituency" in the state.

Arthur Troilo remembers feeling "rather depressed" the morning after Ford's Texas debacle. Steve Bartlett, unable to wrap his mind around his utter failure as a Ford delegate, called his best friend Wick Allison, a young Dallas conservative who was the publisher and cofounder of *D Magazine*. "I asked, 'Wick, how could this have happened? I campaigned. I have more friends than that,'" Bartlett says. "Wick said, 'Are you crazy? I didn't vote for you. You were on the wrong side.'"

The day after the primary, Tower paid a midday visit to the White House and talked with Ford about what went wrong in Texas. At an Indianapolis press conference, a smiling Reagan said he was "still a little stunned" over what had just transpired.

Barry Goldwater, Reagan's philosophical inspiration, suggested on NBC's "Meet the Press" that Reagan's Texas win would have a damaging effect on the GOP because the party was in danger of rupturing. "I think the Republican Party is going through pretty much the same thing it went through when I was running," Goldwater said. "If that kind of division keeps on across this country then I'm afraid the Republican Party is going to have a hard time electing whoever they nominate in November."[61]

In a May 7 letter to Ford, Goldwater attempted to give the president some campaign advice, doing it with the spare-no-feelings bluntness that had become his trademark. "Your speeches are a little bit too long. Get a good speech that is short and use it and use it and use it," Goldwater wrote, adding, in somewhat contradictory fashion, "For God's sake, get off of Panama, but don't let Reagan off that hook."[62]

An internal Ford campaign memo written immediately after the Texas primary described the results as "puzzling," but pinned most of the blame for the defeat on extremist forces outside the party, almost certainly including the ACU in that equation. The memo attributed the high turnout to "skillful organization by extreme right-wing political groups in the Reagan camp operating invisibly through direct mail and voter-turnout efforts conducted by the organizations themselves."[63]

The memo added, in words that could just as easily be applied to the current Tea Party movement: "Many of the members of these groups are not loyal Republicans or Democrats. They are alienated from both parties because neither takes a sympathetic view toward their issues." The memo said these political outsiders had a "rule or ruin" attitude toward the GOP, and concluded: "We are in real danger of being out-organized by a small number of right-wing nuts who are using funds outside of the Reagan campaign expenditure limits."

Reagan rode his Texas momentum to victories in Indiana,

Alabama, and Georgia. All of these states allowed crossover voting, and the formula Reagan had perfected in Texas for attracting Democrats to his cause made all the difference. Ford came back with a big win in his native Michigan and the race ultimately settled into two counterpunching heavyweights trading blows in the center of the ring.

Meanwhile, Texas Republicans wondered if all the new voters they'd attracted on May 1 would stay in the fold. Had their ranks suddenly expanded or had they received a one-time cult-of-personality bump? Most political experts chose the latter, but Angelo and Barnhart had been waiting for years to build the party in their own conservative image, and in June they'd start to get their chance.

CHAPTER 12

A NEW AND INTRANSIGENT REGIME

When Reagan's supporters arrived at the State Republican Convention in Fort Worth, they were in no mood to be magnanimous. Many of them felt that they'd been treated with contempt for months, and now they had all the power.

Barbara Staff still sounds angry at the thought of how GOP party leaders in Texas responded to Reagan's primary win. "I went to a women's council meeting and they practically threw us out. You'd think I was a leech. People really took it offensively that we had such a good campaign against the incumbent," she says.

The first—and biggest—order of business was deciding on the state's four at-large delegates, who would represent the state at the RNC, alongside the ninety-six delegates chosen in the May 1 primary. Ray Barnhart quickly made it clear that the delegate selection would not be a "social award" and wouldn't be handed out as a way of honoring the party's entrenched leaders. He wanted delegates who would be able to go up to the RNC and persuade uncommitted delegates from other states to join the Reagan cause.

Although he was the state party chairman, Ray Hutchison knew that Reagan people didn't want him as a delegate, so he preempted their rejection by announcing that he would not accept an at-large spot. Tower and Connally, the two biggest Republican names in the state, wanted to be at-large delegates, but Barnhart put a stiff condition on the prize. "I went to both Connally and Tower and told them I'd like to have them as at-large delegates, on one condition. They'd have to agree to vote for Reagan on the first three ballots [at the RNC], in conformity with our rules. And each one said they were bigger than that. So I said, 'There's no way in hell you're going to be a delegate to the convention.' They took it bitterly. Some of the folks said I refused to name them, but it was their choice, not mine. But I wasn't going to let them depart from what our state rules were."

The Reagan forces had two-thirds of the 1,674 delegates at the state convention, and they fully intended to use their superior numbers. Angelo challenged venerable state representative Fred Agnich for a spot on the Republican National Committee, and Agnich—who had maintained his neutrality during the Reagan-Ford primary campaign—stepped aside to avoid a bloodbath. Veteran party shaker Pat Archer, the wife of Houston congressman Bill Archer, did the same. Reagan delegate John Leedom, a Dallas city councilman, tried to make it up to Agnich by nominating him for an at-large delegate slot, and Agnich appeased the Reagan forces by promising to support Reagan over Ford. Even after Agnich humbled himself in this way, however, the Reagan army was not satisfied and instead picked J. Evetts Haley—a seventy-four-year-old John Birch Society member who had penned a trashy mid-'60s exposé on Lyndon Johnson. In a way, it was beginning to look like a schoolyard brawl in which one kid backs away at the last minute and throws up his hands, and the other one is too charged up to stop himself from attacking.

Ray Hutchison went into the convention determined to give Reagan supporters whatever they wanted. On the eve of the convention, he told the *Dallas Morning News*, "The main thing that's going to come out of this convention is the feeling by the Reagan people that they have indeed won. No one in any form is going to attempt to deny them the emoluments of that."[64]

A silent fury built up inside of many establishment party members, however, when they looked at all the political experience and know-how this bunch of irascible ideologues had kicked to the curb in the name of conservative purity. John Tower, John Connally, Ray Hutchison, and Fred Agnich were among the most respected names in the party, or at least they had been, as the party had been constituted for years. In this new Texas GOP, Ray Barnhart and Ernest Angelo called the shots, and loyalty to Reagan was prized above prominence and experience.

Shirley Green could hardly believe that Tower, the state's dominant Republican voice, was subjected to a loyalty test that everyone knew he could not pass. "I thought it was outrageous then and I think it's outrageous now," Green says of Tower's exclusion from the state's national delegation. "That's the prime example of how zealous the Reagan people were."

Things got so ugly that one Dallas County Reagan delegate complained to *Texas Monthly* that his fellow Reagan supporters seemed to be on some irrational mission to elevate themselves by destroying the party. "We Reaganites are doing exactly what McGovern's kamikaze people did in 1972 when they shut out labor leaders, party regulars, and [Chicago mayor] Richard Daley," the delegate said.[65]

Among the four at-large delegates selected were Ron Paul—who, as the delegation's highest-ranking elected official, became its nominal head—and energy guru Michael Halbouty. "It was very tricky at the state convention," remembers Polly Sowell, "because Ray Barnhart had been the leader of the Reagan movement, and he was very strong and very loud and very active. He continually had groups of protesters and gathered up people to do various and sundry things. He loved making speeches. So he was out front, big time, for Reagan."

After observing the tense opening-day state committee meeting, *Dallas Morning News* political analyst Robert Baskin was struck by what he called the party's "new and intransigent regime" of Reagan diehards. Describing the gathering as "one of the sourest Texas Republican conventions ever held in recent memory," Baskin bashed those in the Reagan camp "who consider it their obligation to rout the opposition completely, no matter what the consequences" to the GOP. "I always thought you had to be magnanimous in victory," one Ford delegate said, in a quote lifted from Winston Churchill. "But there is not the least sign of it here."[66]

A sign above the podium at the Tarrant County Convention Center said, "Together We Can." Whether it was positive projection or wishful thinking, the sign reflected the artificial nature of the truce in the hall. Ford supporters had agreed to bite their tongues, to silently carry their resentments so that no explosive confrontations would emerge. It was coexistence, but not harmony. If Hutchison and the rest of the state party leadership wanted unity, this would have to do.

On Saturday, June 19, the Texas GOP trotted out its big—albeit embattled—guns. John Tower took the stage after a polite but not particularly effusive introduction by Ernest Angelo. Tower saved his most impassioned lines for Jimmy Carter, who he said was offering a platform that constituted a "blueprint for socialism." But he also directly addressed the five-ton Republican elephant in the room: his intense support for Ford, and the hard feelings it had caused in the Texas GOP. He even drew two hearty rounds of applause when he promised to vigorously support the party's presidential nominee, regardless of who it turned out to be. "I implore you to subordinate any bitterness you may have . . . toward the greater goal of ensuring not only victory for the Republican Party, but for the country in November."[67]

Tower was overshadowed at the state convention, as he so often was, by his old nemesis John Connally. Connally managed to break the spell of a weekend in which delegates spent the bulk of their time bursting into theatrical applause every time Ronald Reagan's name was mentioned. Connally's attacks on congressional Democrats—who had ruled Capitol Hill for twenty-eight of the last thirty-two years at that point—and his insistence, against all odds, that 1976 would be a "golden year" for the GOP earned him a standing ovation and only intensified calls for him to be on the GOP ticket that fall.

On Saturday afternoon, the convention adopted a set of platform resolutions, which they planned to take to the national convention two months later in Kansas City. It was a hard-line set of principles that the GOP's right wing has been running on—if not always governing on—ever since. If someone went looking for a proto–Tea Party document in the maze of 1970s American politics, this would be their ideal destination. The resolutions called for a constitutional amendment blocking Congress from increasing the national debt, except in cases of national emergency; strict term limits for Congress and one six-year term for the president; more incentives for oil exploration and increased development of nuclear energy; a constitutional amendment prohibiting abortion; the states to take responsibility for their own environmental concerns away from the federal government; children of undocumented immigrants to be prohibited from attending public schools and disqualified from attaining US citizenship; and opposition to any national health insurance program.

At the same time that conservatives were consolidating their hold on the state GOP, liberals were flexing their strength at the

Democratic State Convention in Houston. Historically, whenever walkouts occurred at Texas Democratic gatherings, it usually had been liberals venting their frustration over the iron-handed domination of the party by conservatives. In 1976, the roles reversed themselves, as a group of eighty Dallas conservatives stormed out in anger after twenty-four conservative at-large delegates were unseated. The conservative delegates were replaced by twenty-two Jimmy Carter backers and two uncommitted liberals.

At least one longtime party leader voiced what many Democrats were thinking: that the Bentsen Primary Bill had inadvertently pulled conservatives over to the GOP tent and given liberals much greater power in the Democratic Party. "These liberals are kicking out conservatives who were duly elected," said Earl Luna, a veteran party official. "Bentsen's primary bill did it. There just aren't many of us conservatives left."[68]

CHAPTER 13

KANSAS CITY DREAMING

If dominating the state convention temporarily knocked the chip off the shoulder of Reagan's Texas army, that chip reappeared as a boulder two months later when delegates arrived in Kansas City for the Republican National Convention.

The convention was being held at the then-new Kemper Arena, a building created to house the Kansas City Kings, an NBA basketball franchise that would later relocate to Sacramento. Kemper Arena was located in the heart of downtown Kansas City, but the accommodations for the all-Reagan Texas delegation were nowhere close to downtown Kansas City. They were nearly twenty miles away, across the Missouri state line, at the Glenwood Manor Motor Hotel in Overland Park, Kansas. To their way of thinking, this was a calculated act of dirty pool on the part of the Ford-controlled Republican National Committee. "The party hierarchy didn't want us closer, because they didn't want us to be any more effective than that," Ernest Angelo says.

"Anytime they could give us the shaft, they usually did," Ray Barnhart says. "I just had a conniption about it, because here we had two hundred delegates and alternates, and [the RNC] put us up at that hotel. They said, 'Don't worry about it. We will have buses to carry you down to the convention center.' I thought, 'Yeah, you'll probably have one every forty-five minutes.'" Barnhart was so distrustful of the RNC that he leased buses from Texas to transport the delegation to and from the convention. "It's a good thing we did," he adds, "because they [the RNC] would have screwed us."

Fortunately for Barnhart and Angelo, their banker pal Jimmy Lyon was a member of the GOP's national platform committee and needed to be in Kansas City a week before the convention. Lyon was more than willing to splurge on a downtown Kansas City hotel suite, and that suite became the unofficial command central for Reagan followers. It drew so much attention that CBS News ultimately devoted a segment to the buzz of convention activity developing around it. "Jimmy went up there early," Barnhart says.

> I didn't have any money, but I went up anyway, because I was talking to Lyn Nofziger on the phone and telling him that I was afraid some of our [Texas] people weren't going to have the balls to face up to some of the stuff going on [at the convention]. He said, "If you're so damn smart, get off your butt and get up here." So I did. Jimmy and I shared a room. [The Reagan campaign] didn't have all the communication the Ford people had: the walkie-talkies and everything else. So I would provide sandwiches at noon, and they'd all flock in there. That's how we kept everything going with the campaign, and how we were coping with all the sophisticated stuff from the Ford campaign.

Barnhart, Angelo, and Lyon also used the suite as a conference room to bring in uncommitted delegates, as well as those whose commitment to Ford seemed shaky, and try to work some friendly Texas persuasion on them.

In the weeks leading up to the convention, Ford's slim but significant delegate lead seemed to be solidifying, and the Reagan camp sensed that some of their national support—under hard-sell pressure from the White House—might be eroding. With the kind of high-risk, high-reward bravado he was known for, Sears came up with an inspired gimmick. He persuaded Reagan to name liberal Pennsylvania senator Richard Schweiker as his running mate—in the event that Reagan won the nomination. On Monday, July 26— three weeks before the national convention—Reagan announced his veep selection at a brief Los Angeles press conference.

This name-your-running-mate-before-you've-won stuff was new political territory, and Sears hoped that the Schweiker bombshell would not only steal media attention away from Ford but also pry loose some Northeastern moderate and liberal delegates. The first part of the plan worked well enough, but Schweiker didn't have much success—even with his home-state delegation—at per- suading Ford delegates to switch sides. Additionally, much of the attention that the Schweiker announcement received was nega- tive. Many of Reagan's most ardent conservative supporters, par- ticularly in the South, viewed this ticket-balancing maneuver as a cynical betrayal. Texas senator Betty Andujar spoke for more than a few Reaganites when she said, "We're keenly disappointed at [Reagan's] choice. We want John Connally in the number-two position on our ticket."

Connally, who'd been waiting for a convenient time to throw his support behind Ford, exploited the fallout from the Schweiker announcement without mentioning it directly. On Tuesday, July 27, he stood by Ford's side at the White House's Rose Garden and called the president "unmistakably the better choice" in the GOP race. The Mississippi delegation had been pledged as a unit to Reagan, but the Schweiker announcement had discombobulated Clarke Reed, their anxious, profoundly indecisive state chairman. As the convention approached, Reed vacillated on a nearly hourly basis between Reagan and Ford, and often looked like he was on the verge of a nervous breakdown.

With time running out and the numbers on Ford's side, Sears settled on a last-ditch plan to steal delegates away from the president. He reasoned correctly that Reagan's emotional appeal was stronger than Ford's and surmised that some delegates pledged to Ford secretly preferred Reagan. Sears believed that if he could stir up a floor fight over some issue, any issue, he had a chance to throw the whole process off-kilter. Some Ford delegates who were committed to vote for the president on the first ballot might abstain and switch to Reagan on the second ballot.

While many Reagan diehards wanted to pick a fight over a deep ideological concern, Sears opted for a procedural issue. He proposed a new party rule—which would come to be known as 16-C— requiring presidential candidates to disclose their vice presidential selection in advance of the party's roll-call vote for president. Two days before the convention opened, Rule 16-C was shot down by the party's rules committee, but by receiving more than 25 percent of the vote, the issue made it to the convention floor, just as Sears had hoped. It shaped up to be the central battle of the convention's second night and the last chance for Reagan to break Ford's stranglehold before the convention picked its presidential nominee.

Even Reagan supporters who understood Sears's logic thought 16-C was fundamentally unworthy of a floor fight. If the battle had been over Henry Kissinger or the Panama Canal, sure, but why force a presidential candidate to tip his hand so quickly on a running mate? The practical effect of the rule was that GOP presidential contenders would subsequently be prevented from naming one of their opponents as a running mate, because no one still clinging to hope for the presidential nomination would ever accept the number-two slot. "We didn't like 16-C," Angelo says. "Our delegation was threatening to mutiny over supporting it. Ray [Barnhart] and I had a real knock-down drag-out with them on the floor of the convention that day, and, between us, we talked to the ones that were the most recalcitrant. We told them, 'You've spent this whole time working for [Reagan], and now the first thing that comes up, it's a key vote. It may be a dumb vote, but it's our vote and you've got to vote for it.' Well, they did."

As tension mounted in the arena, CBS reporter Dan Rather announced on the air that the Texas caucus was considering bolting from Reagan to Ford. For Barnhart, who saw his delegation as a group of idealistic insurgents taking on the entrenched, all-powerful status quo, this was almost too much to take. He knew that he could hold Texas together for Reagan, and he thought Rather was recklessly undermining that effort. "Rather was making a statement on the floor, which Ray and I overheard, about friction in the Texas delegation," Angelo says. "Ray confronted Rather immediately after that, with me to back him up. Rather was sheepish about it, but he didn't apologize."

True to form, Barnhart's memory of the incident is considerably more dramatic and colorful. In his telling, he's not the instigator, but rather the peacemaker. "I got on the floor and word had been passed to the delegation that Rather had made that statement," Barnhart says. "And three or four of our guys took off looking for Rather and were going to beat the hell out of him. I thought, 'That's all we need!'"

Barnhart says he ran to the CBS booth, hoping to warn Rather about the impending beat-down. He says a guard outside the booth refused to let him in, but a couple of Barnhart's friends were able to divert the guard long enough for Barnhart to sneak inside the booth and tell CBS reps to alert Rather. "They found out where Rather was and told him just to stay there hidden. We went over and got him and I explained to him that nobody in the Texas delegation wanted to abandon Reagan. He said, 'What do I do about it?' I said, 'I think you better come down and explain this to the Texas delegation and apologize.'"

Barnhart says he remembers Rather standing up on a chair and offering a mea culpa to the Texas delegation while Barnhart and his cohorts heartily sang "The Eyes of Texas." Barnhart's ability to spin a yarn was matched only by his willingness to mix it up with the Ford forces.

The Texas delegation had been positioned in the back corner of the convention hall. They were directly below the Ford family, which sat along the front row of the balcony, joined by singer Tony Orlando, a loyal Ford supporter. On the opening night of the convention, Texas delegates pointedly refused to stand when Betty Ford made her convention entrance right above them. They took a similar tack that night when Vice President Rockefeller addressed the convention, a snub that made Ron Paul—no admirer of Rocky himself—uncomfortable. "When Rockefeller was introduced, most people stood up, out of respect," says Paul, who brought along his thirteen-year-old son Rand, now a Republican senator from Kentucky, to the convention. "Our delegation did not stand up, but I did. I remember somebody showing me a picture later on, and everybody was sitting on their hands. They asked me, 'Why are you standing up for this guy?' I said, 'Out of respect for the office, I guess.'"

Rockefeller, in what amounted to his last hurrah, refused to slink away quietly, goading right-wingers in the hall for shrinking the party's base. The GOP, Rockefeller said, needed candidates that "appealed to the broad spectrum of the American populace, not a narrow few." Reagan delegates roundly booed that suggestion.

Even though the nomination wouldn't be officially decided until Wednesday night, Tuesday was the critical night for the '76 convention. Tuesday was the night for the Rule 16-C vote, and a Ford victory on that rule would essentially seal his nomination.

John Connally, still identified as a possible veep selection for Ford, was the featured speaker on Tuesday. With anticipation building for the 16-C vote, Vincent Cianci, mayor of Providence, Rhode Island, strode to the podium and launched into a fawning introduction of the former Texas governor. Cianci noted that Connally "grew up among the Polish, Mexican, and Czechoslovakian communities of South Texas," and called him "a man whose wisdom and judgment has been sought by four presidents." Connally, he assured the delegates, was "one of us." The Texas delegation, which was already developing a reputation for cold-shouldering anyone connected with the Ford campaign, could have done the same to Connally. But in a fit of pure state loyalty, they waved Texas banners and hollered with gusto for Big John.

Connally faced the tough task of making a case for a Republican presidential nominee, when that nominee had not yet been chosen by the convention. His winding and weaving thirty-five-minute speech certainly showed the strain. In the oddly formal dialect of a Texas farm boy mimicking his idea of an eloquent nineteenth-century politician (e.g., the way he perpetually pronounced the word "again" as "a-gain"), Connally began innocuously by tapping into the bicentennial spirit of the summer. The GOP of 1976, Connally said, was just like the Founding Fathers of 1776. Both groups were "debating together, contesting together, and deciding together."

Before long, Connally veered into a dark apocalyptic tunnel, saying that the United States, like the empires of Egypt, Greece, and Rome, could be facing extinction. As the crowd grew audibly restless, Connally warned them: "We must tell the American people that we have seen the end of an era of abundance and affluence, and indeed now face a period of scarcity and sacrifice."

This message might have accurately reflected the creeping American sense that austerity was the answer and limitations must be accepted. It was hard to see, however, how it did the GOP's incumbent president any favors. It was also completely at odds with the vision that Reagan carried to the convention (and would ultimately carry to the presidency). More than anything else, Connally's speech illustrated how two fundamentally conservative politicians could sing the same song in radically different registers.

Connally did break ground with at least one part of his speech, even if it escaped the attention of many delegates that night. He pointedly refused to refer to the opposition—which happened to be his former political base—as the "Democratic Party," instead branding them the "Democrat Party." It was a distinction that the GOP would not universally embrace until the 1980s, but, as with term limits, Connally was ahead of the curve.

After Connally splashed a bucket of cold pessimism on the assembled delegates, something suspiciously resembling a spontaneous demonstration erupted on the floor. By 1976, network television coverage had induced the major parties to turn their conventions into carefully choreographed advertisements for their candidates. Certainly, Nixon's 1972 coronation bash at Miami Beach had been the ultimate example of that. In 1976, however, the Republicans were too emotionally divided to stay on message, and the '76 RNC now stands as the last of the old-style open conventions. It marked the last time a presidential nomination was still up for grabs at the convention, and the last time a major party dared to expose its conflicted soul so deeply to a prime-time audience. In the words of CBS anchor Walter Cronkite: "[It was] one of the rip-roaringest Republican conventions in the memory of modern man." Jeff Bell recalls it as "Armageddon, just incomparable in terms of the intensity and the emotion."

Delegates brought the convention to a halt with competing chants for Ford and Reagan, and temporary convention chairman Bob Dole spent much of Tuesday night haplessly pounding his gavel in a futile attempt to bring order to the proceedings. Things didn't calm down until the convention band kicked into an abbreviated version of "God Bless America."

Shortly before 16-C was set to come up for a vote, Nancy Reagan entered the hall with eighteen-year-old son Ron Jr., and Reagan delegates once again exploded with joy. That's when the convention's most bizarre moment occurred. As Nancy waved to her adoring throng below, the band inexplicably kicked into the schmaltzy chorus of "Tie a Yellow Ribbon Round the Ole Oak Tree," Tony Orlando's chart-topping 1973 hit. In response, Orlando and Betty Ford launched into a hammy dance in front of their seats, while John Connally stood one row behind, clapping in time. As he watched Orlando and Betty Ford spin each other around in a forced display of camera-ready giddiness, Connally wore the sad, crooked grin of a man who'd just returned from three hours of painful orthodontic work.

Betty Ford's obvious attempt to upstage Nancy Reagan flabbergasted network news commentators. As the band belatedly segued into "California Here I Come," NBC went to a split screen of the two candidates' wives simultaneously vying for the attention and affection of the Republican Party. "I don't think I've ever seen anything like this," NBC anchor John Chancellor said to David Brinkley. Ray Barnhart responded by telling the *Dallas Morning News* it was "really crass and in poor taste" for the First Lady to be "dancing a jig" with Orlando while Nancy Reagan was acknowledging the cheers of Reagan supporters. Barbara Staff called the dance routine a "low, cheap shot."[69]

Orlando was also at the center of a convention incident that

Texas delegates continue to grumble about. In the middle of a pro-Ford celebration on Thursday night, Orlando and Jack Ford dumped an airline bag's worth of toilet paper, trash, and confetti over the balcony, directly on the Texas delegation. "We were right under the Ford box, up against the wall," Ernest Angelo says. "They dumped all kinds of trash on us. When it started coming down, it landed on the back of the delegation. They were laughing upstairs, and Mrs. Ford was laughing. It was so crass that it was unbeliev-able." The incident was the culmination of a testy week between the Texas delegation and the Ford family. Some Texas delegates had made a ritual of antagonizing the first family (and Jack Ford in particular) at the convention, loudly heckling them with epi-thets such as "I smell marijuana, so the Ford family must be around here."[70]

In his autobiography, *Halfway to Paradise*, Orlando revealed that the 1976 convention coincided with a dark period of cocaine abuse for him. He said he remembered the infamous dance with Betty Ford, but "the rest of the convention is a blur in my memory." In a possible hint that he let his pro-Ford partisanship get out of hand in Kansas City, he added, "You never feel as competitive and anx-ious about a 'contest' as you do with something that will possibly determine who the next president of the United States will be."[71]

Sears had hoped that some Ford delegates would vote for 16-C because they wanted to know who Ford planned to name as his running mate before the Wednesday night roll call. Thanks to the expert delegate wrangling of James Baker, a veteran Houston pol who had handled George Bush's failed 1970 Senate campaign, defections from the Ford camp were minimal, and they were nearly matched by Reaganites who hated the concept of 16-C and voted against it.

By the time the 16-C roll call came to Texas, Ford had 999 votes (out of the 1,130 he needed for a majority), while Reagan had 832. If the Reagan forces were feeling downcast, however, you saw no evidence of it in Ray Barnhart. Wearing a dark suit and a white cowboy hat with "Reagan" printed in blue letters on the brim, Barnhart leaned into the microphone and proclaimed to the nation: "The state of Texas casts one hundred principled votes—Aye!" As the Reagan diehards in the arena let out a thunderous roar, Barnhart, flanked by Angelo and Halbouty, busted out an ear-to-ear grin, shouted "Hey!" to no one in particular, and started exuberantly waving his hat around.

Despite such cheerleading displays, Ford's win on 16-C (by a margin of 1,180 to 1,068) left little doubt that he would be able to secure the nomination on the first ballot. That night, Barnhart and Angelo returned to their hotel suite and began brainstorming. There had to be some way out, some way to pull off a last-second miracle. They made a late-night phone call to New Hampshire governor Meldrim Thompson, who was spending the convention week in his home state. As Barnhart, Angelo, and Thompson rolled around all the possibilities, they all agreed on a plan to win the nomination: Reagan had to dump Schweiker from the ticket. That way he could reassure conservatives, lock down the Mississippi delegation, and steal enough uncommitted delegates to make the difference.

It was a bleary-eyed shot in the dark from two tired Texas refuseniks who had hardly slept all week. After pulling an all-nighter, Barnhart and Angelo showed up at Reagan's Alameda Plaza Hotel suite Wednesday morning at the crack of dawn. "Reagan came out in his bathrobe," Angelo says. "We told him about our plan, and he stopped us in the middle of it, almost in anger. He said, 'Hold it, fellas, I don't want to hear any more.' He told us what a fine man Schweiker was, and said, 'If you had the power to guarantee me the nomination [by dumping Schweiker], I still wouldn't do it.'" Angelo remembers feeling slightly embarrassed as he and Barnhart wearily left Reagan's suite, but he also sensed the real affection Reagan had for them in the muted way he explained why their idea was out of the question.

Wednesday night, in a final act of pent-up defiance, California and Texas—two large delegations passionately in the Reagan column—began chanting across the hall at each other. Nobody knew how it started, but before long, California delegates were shouting "Viva" and Texans were shouting back "Olé," and the convention ground to a halt. Ron Paul calls it his most vivid memory of the '76 convention experience. "We had a great time with that. It ticked off the Ford people, no question about it," Barnhart says.

"They had California stuck in a corner on the other side, which turned out to be a mistake because they would shout on their side, and we'd shout on ours," Angelo says. "It became the Reagan cheer. We shut things down, almost out of frustration or meanness."

Even Barnhart and Angelo knew they couldn't shut the convention down forever, and before the night was done, Gerald Ford had secured one of the most hard-earned victories in American political history, with 1,187 delegates to 1,070 for Reagan. A fourth of Reagan's delegate total had come from two states: Texas and California. If 60 delegates had gone the other way, Reagan would have been the one celebrating Wednesday night.

Late in the evening, Ford paid a visit to Reagan at the Alameda Plaza, and the two erstwhile warriors had a cordial twenty-seven-minute exchange. Reagan had already made it clear that he wanted no part of the vice presidency, and Ford didn't ask. They discussed other VP candidates, and Reagan gave his blessing to Bob Dole, the man Ford selected Thursday morning. Dole won easy confirmation from the convention Thursday night. Ray Barnhart received one vote for vice president, but then again, so did Dallas Cowboys quarterback Roger Staubach.

John Tower played a key role in Ford's running-mate selection process (interestingly, he pushed hard in the final hours for Connally, his longtime Texas rival), but he was a sad, exiled figure in Kansas City. He watched much of the proceedings from a Kemper Arena sky box, silently stewing as he looked down on the rambunctious Texas delegation from which he'd been excluded. Of course, Tower's relationship with Texas Republicans was never neat and simple, and while some Texas Reaganites wanted nothing to do with the pint-sized senator who'd been so dismissive of their candidate, others openly complained that Tower was ignoring them even while he found time to visit with Mississippi delegates. "A lot of the delegates are upset over Tower going to the Mississippi delegation," said Lila Rehkop, a delegate from Athens, Texas. "We think he ought to be out here. He's our senator, and I miss him."[72]

In a brazen shot at Tower—and a show of loyalty to the chairman of their delegation—some Texas delegates periodically shouted from the convention floor that Barnhart should run for Tower's Senate seat in 1978. It was an idea that Barnhart didn't initiate but didn't exactly discourage. *Dallas Morning News* columnist Robert Baskin observed such antics from the Texas delegation and concluded, "The Reagan people are a strange crowd. They have demonstrated a vindictive spirit that is not in the best traditions of either the Republican Party or the American political system."[73]

On the final night of the convention, Pat Boone opened the proceedings by crooning the national anthem, and screen legend Cary Grant made a rare public appearance with a brief introductory speech for his friend Betty Ford. But the speech that really counted Thursday night came from the president. With his political future depending on it, Ford delivered a workman-like, meat-

and-potatoes acceptance speech with a winning feistiness, as if he felt so relieved to be liberated from Reagan's right-wing attacks that he could barely contain his eagerness to play the conservative attack-dog role against Jimmy Carter. It was easily his best public-speaking performance as president.

As the balloons rained down and the Ford family joined the president at the podium for a curtain-closing victory lap, Ford made an unconventional move in the name of party unity. He not only surprised Reagan by inviting him up to the podium; he took it further by asking him to address the delegates.

This was unprecedented territory: the nominee of his party, a sitting president, willingly became the opening act for his van-quished challenger's headliner performance. It may have been the one mistake Ford made that night. Reagan spoke for less than six minutes, but he made his time count. Just as he had first done during the Texas campaign, he made a point of connecting—at this most partisan of Republican events—with people outside the GOP tent. "I'm going to say 'fellow Republicans here,' but those that are watching from a distance, all those millions of Democrats and independents who I know are looking for a cause around which to rally and which I believe we can give them," Reagan said.

As his loyalists fought back tears, Reagan told them the conven-tion "will give us a memory that will live in our hearts forever." Abruptly, he broke into a story about a letter he'd recently been asked to write for a time capsule that would be opened in Los Angeles in one hundred years. "Those who would read this letter one hundred years from now . . . will know whether we met our challenge. Whether they have the freedoms that we have known up until now will depend on what we do here. Will they look back with appreciation and say, 'Thank God for those people in 1976 who headed off that loss of freedom'?"

It was a rare instance of party members getting a sample taste of what the losing candidate might have been like as the nominee. Even on Ford's best night, he couldn't compete with Reagan's assurance, his practiced ease, and his ability to make a political campaign feel like a crusade. Almost instantly, many delegates in the room felt buyer's remorse. If Reagan's 1964 Goldwater address was The Speech, this impromptu call to arms was The Moment, the instant in which the entire Republican Party melted in the face of Reagan's charisma offensive. He would never again be seen by a significant segment of this party as a reckless extremist or the leader of a fringe movement. Ford was the nominee, but Reagan now owned the GOP.

For Barnhart and Angelo, it had been a long, hard slog. Both of them had spent nearly a year working to get Reagan elected, and in the process they'd almost completely abandoned their companies. "I was essentially spending all my time either being mayor of Midland or running Reagan's campaign," Angelo says. "It's a miracle that my business didn't go under. Ray pretty well did lose his business. He gave everything he had to the cause, and it really cost him dearly."

Barnhart concedes that the campaign was financially devastating to him. When his underground-utilities business went under, he rebounded by jumping into the insurance business, working as an agent for the Houston-based Barmore Insurance Agency. "It was tough," he says, "because I didn't have any money and I never charged the campaign for anything. I wasn't there with the big rich. Of course, I'd alienated some people, but I didn't regret it, nor did my family, because we were all very fond of Reagan."

Ford's spirited acceptance speech, and the final-night show of unity at the convention, helped him close Jimmy Carter's thirty-point lead in the polls down to a manageable ten, almost overnight. Carter gave him opportunities, particularly an ill-considered *Playboy* interview in which he revealed that he'd often "lusted in his heart" for women other than his wife. But Ford couldn't capitalize. Going into their second debate, at a moment when the race looked like Ford's to win, the president defended his foreign policy by making the bewilderingly inaccurate statement that there was "no Soviet domination of Eastern Europe, and there never will be under a Ford administration." Once again, Ford had made himself the object of ridicule, and his campaign never fully recovered.

On Tuesday, November 2, Carter won a narrow victory, taking 50 percent of the popular vote to 48 percent for Ford, with a shaky electoral-vote margin of 297 to 240. Ultimately, seventeen thousand votes in Ohio and Hawaii made the difference between victory and defeat for Carter.

Carter carried Texas by a thin margin, but the state could have been winnable for Ford if his campaign team had better utilized the Reagan forces. As it turned out, the distrust that had built up between the two sides was not easy to erase in a matter of weeks. "They [the Ford campaign] turned the cold shoulder on me," Barnhart says. "They were quite nasty, as a matter of fact. I volunteered to do what I could to help them and they just shunted me aside. I didn't care, quite frankly, 'cause I didn't think that highly of Jerry Ford."

It should have been a golden time for Texas Democrats. As many of them had hoped, the Democratic Party had won back the White House by turning to a Southern moderate who'd been able to retake Dixie from the GOP. But the walkout of conservative Democrats at the June state convention suggested that even entrenched party activists were beginning to feel the pull of Reagan's crusade. Their marriage of convenience with liberal Democrats was turning sour and heading for an acrimonious divorce.

CHAPTER 14

WHAT IF?

Viewed from a retrospective distance, almost every election result tends to look like it was inevitable. For instance, you could say that John Kennedy was the fated choice in 1960 because the nation was saying farewell to Dwight Eisenhower, the oldest American president up to that time, and was eager for a shot of youthful vitality. You could also argue that Bill Clinton was destined to win the presidency in 1992 because he made the economy the central issue of the campaign, and voters sensed that George Bush was disengaged from the nation's economic problems.

In truth, Kennedy's margin of victory came down to a few votes in some historically shady precincts in Illinois and Texas, and almost certainly had more to do with old-school machine politics than the bright promise of a New Frontier. In Clinton's case, all of his I-feel-your-pain empathy for those suffering in a slow economy might have meant nothing if Dallas billionaire Ross Perot hadn't monkey-wrenched Bush's prospects by garnering nearly 20 million votes as an independent candidate.

No American presidency of the last fifty years feels more inevitable than Ronald Reagan's, partly because he was twice elected in overwhelming landslides, and partly because his persona is as inextricable from our collective memory of the 1980s as the Rubik's

Cube or Michael Jackson's single crystal-beaded glove. Reagan's election in 1980, however, would be much harder to imagine if Gerald Ford had been able to ride John Tower's support to victory in the 1976 Texas primary, or if Democrats in the Texas legislature had not created a '76 presidential primary in the first place.

There's little doubt that Texas represented Reagan's final Hail Mary pass of the '76 campaign. Reagan campaign manager John Sears had publicly stated that the campaign needed a win in Texas to remain viable, and Reagan had privately agreed with Sears that a loss in Texas left the campaign with no plausible path to the nomination. A Reagan defeat in Texas would have meant an early exit from the GOP race after having lost nine of ten primaries to Ford. Reagan would have been viewed as a man who stirred up division in his party and then failed miserably in his challenge to the incumbent. If Ted Kennedy was forever weakened by his bungled intraparty campaign against Jimmy Carter in 1980, at least he could say that he finished strongly and took his fight all the way to the convention. A defeat in Texas would have left Reagan no such argument.

After losing to Carter in the '76 general election, Ford wanted to run again in 1980. In fact, he privately seethed over the fact that Reagan didn't step aside and let the former president get another crack at Carter in 1980. With Reagan in a strong position going into 1980, Ford opted to stay out of the race, but the dynamic would have been completely different if Reagan had been knocked out after the '76 Texas primary. Ford, who was convinced that he could beat Carter in a rematch, would have been a likely front-runner in a crowded 1980 GOP field. In fact, Ford later suggested that he could have beaten Carter in '76 if his candidacy had not been mortally wounded by the major expenditures of effort, time, and money that went into fending off Reagan's challenge for the nomination.

While political insiders often make the case that a tough primary battle is a blessing in disguise because it sharpens a candidate's stump skills, that argument simply didn't apply to Ford.

The overriding lesson that Ford's political advisers took from the '76 primary campaign was that the harder Ford worked on the campaign trail, the worse he did. At his best, he was a bland, enervating speaker; at his worst, he would try too hard and turn painfully strident. People generally found the *idea* of Ford comforting, but the reality of watching him at close range often resulted in the most common critique he faced as president: He's a nice guy, but he's in over his head.

Ford did best under the most controlled circumstances, which made him ideal for a Rose Garden strategy. If Reagan had lost Texas, Ford could have retreated to the White House in early May and spent the next three and a half months dutifully mending any lingering rifts in the party. He also could have avoided the public, intraparty battering he took over détente, America's military preparedness, and the Panama Canal. That battering enabled Carter to effectively use Reagan's words against Ford, pointing out in the second fall debate that Ford increased military spending only after Reagan made it a central issue in Texas.

Ford's central plan against Carter was to paint him as a liberal in disguise, an evasive flip-flopper who wanted to be all things to all people, but was secretly George McGovern with a Southern accent. That approach worked up to a point, but because many ardent Reagan conservatives had come to believe that Ford himself was too liberal, they viewed the general election as an unappealing choice between bad and slightly worse.

If Reagan had pulled out of the race after Texas, and Ford had gone on to beat Carter in the fall, Reagan would have faced a different set of obstacles in 1980. Ford would have been constitutionally barred from seeking a second full term in 1980, but Bob Dole, his vice president, would have been an obvious successor.

Coming off a full Ford term, any GOP nominee would have faced a tougher road than the one Reagan ultimately encountered in 1980. Instead of running against Jimmy Carter's spotty record as president, they would have been boxed into either praising Ford or maintaining a diplomatic silence about him (as John McCain did with George W. Bush in 2008). The country would have been at the end of twelve solid years of Republicans in the White House and almost certainly ripe for a change.

In any event, Reagan would have been up against steep odds in 1980 if he'd lost the '76 Texas primary. Already in 1976, Reagan found himself questioned about his age. At sixty-five, he was older than any president had been upon entering the office since William Henry Harrison in 1841—and Harrison died only a month into his presidency. Though Reagan himself never said it, a common perception in 1976 was that when Reagan dared to make the unusual move of challenging an incumbent from his own party, he did so at least partly because his advanced age meant that he wouldn't get another chance.

The age issue dissolved in 1980 because Reagan entered the campaign with so much momentum from 1976—in a sense, he never stopped running during that four-year period—that he was regarded almost as an incumbent. By then, Reagan had an impassioned national base, a strong contingent of disaffected Democrats, and considerable political mystique. All of those elements were built in that four-month window from the Texas primary campaign to the last night of the 1976 Republican National Convention. "Once Ford had lost to Carter, the Texas primary, more than any other event, made Reagan into the front-runner and showed the intensity that he was capable of generating," Jeff Bell says.

If Reagan had dropped out after Texas, his entire 1976 campaign would have been viewed as an ill-considered failure. Under those circumstances, it's almost impossible to imagine Ford inviting him up to the podium to make his famous '76 convention speech. Also, the endorsements and fundraising dollars that flowed his way by the beginning of the 1980 campaign wouldn't necessarily have been there for a candidate who dropped out midway through the '76 primary campaign.

Reagan later said that he was a reluctant candidate in '76 but needed no persuading in 1980. Much of his enthusiasm for another run came from the excitement his insurgent '76 campaign generated down the stretch against Ford and the wildly emotional reception he drew at the convention. It's impossible to know how Reagan would have responded to an early knockout in the '76 race, but, given his age, his comfortable life in California, his lucrative gig as a radio commentator, and his diminished political luster, it's easy to imagine him staying out of the 1980 race altogether. "It was assumed that if he didn't win in '76, he wasn't going to be around for 1980," Steve Munisteri says. "But because that race was close, he was viable in '80. It had to be that close, and with the dramatic ['76 convention] speech that he gave, that's the only way he would have been president. And that was all set up by this 1976 primary. These people [Barnhart and Angelo], in effect, changed history dramatically."

Reagan's stunning triumph in Texas also provided the Texas GOP with its own much-needed catalyst. At the time, young Republican activists across the state were struggling to build a party infrastructure, find candidates for down-ballot races, and get voters interested in their primaries. With one dramatic presidential campaign, Reagan lured tens of thousands of Texas Democrats and political fence-sitters into the GOP fold for a single day, and before long many of them began to identify themselves as Republicans. As Mark Elam points out, "Much of the conservative movement in Texas and nationwide came together during that 1976 Reagan campaign."

With Reagan's boost, the Texas GOP brand went from country club to populist. Reagan became a kind of logo on the stationery, making it acceptable—and even advantageous—for high-profile Democrats to defect. Rick Perry switched parties in 1989, shortly after being elected to his third term as a Democratic state representative. After years of being at odds with his more liberal Democratic colleagues in the legislature, Perry was able to quickly assert himself in the GOP, challenging incumbent Democrat Jim Hightower for state agriculture commissioner in 1990, and coming away with a close, hard-earned victory.

Kent Hance served three terms in the US House of Representatives as a "boll-weevil Democrat" but was too conservative to win the Democratic nomination for the US Senate in 1984. Almost certainly, he would have had a better chance taking on Phil Gramm—another former Democrat—in the Republican primary. Reading the obvious writing on the wall, Hance switched parties in 1985, with a plan to run for governor the following year. (He fell short in both the '86 and '90 gubernatorial primaries.) "I felt very comfortable with Reagan," he says. "I got to know him personally, and he encouraged me. He called me and urged me to switch, and reminded me that at one time he'd been a Democrat and made the change. One time, in the early '80s, he told me, Phil Gramm, and some of the other boll weevils: 'If all the Democrats had been like you all, I'd have never switched.'"

Texas and the Deep South states may have eventually morphed from blue to red even without Reagan because the Republican Party was already making inroads in that part of the country. But the shift wouldn't have been so sweeping and overpowering. It's worth remembering that as far back as 1952, when Eisenhower carried Texas, Republicans in the Lone Star State thought the tide of history was moving in their direction. In the twenty-four years after that breakthrough, however, they'd made remarkably little progress in electing candidates or building a grassroots base. Conservative Democrats in Texas had little reason to abandon a party they controlled for a smaller party long associated with the snooty elite. Reagan, however, made them want to switch.

James Baker served as Ford's campaign chairman in 1976 and ran George H. W. Bush's 1980 presidential campaign before serving as Reagan's White House chief of staff and treasury secretary. "Ronald Reagan gets a lot of credit for that [state realignment]," Baker told the *Houston Chronicle* in 2011. "The whole shape and nature of the state changed."[74]

The '76 Texas primary campaign resonated as far away as New Jersey, where Jeff Bell made a bid for the US Senate in 1978. In his first-ever campaign as a candidate (rather than a behind-the-scenes aide), Bell knocked off a four-term incumbent, liberal Republican Clifford Case, in the primary and gave eventual winner Bill Bradley a respectable contest in the general election. Bell says,

> It was a turning point in my own life, because I got out of the policy-wonk business and decided to become a candidate. If you've been through something as successful as the Reagan Texas primary of May 1976, you start to think you're pretty big stuff. I went from being the goat of the campaign to saying, "You know, I ought to run for something, 'cause I could find the equivalent of Rollie Millirons in New Jersey." I never would have run for the Senate if it weren't for the three and a half weeks I spent in Texas.

CHAPTER 15

★ STANDING IN THE SHADOWS

The three most important figures in the 1978 Texas gubernatorial race were not on the ballot. With the 1980 presidential race around the corner and Texas established as a pivotal state, Ronald Reagan, George H. W. Bush, and John Connally spent much of the gubernatorial campaign standing in the shadows and quietly jockeying for position.

The GOP contest came down to Ray Hutchison, the former state party chair, and Bill Clements, a brash, wealthy Dallas oilman who'd run Nixon's 1972 Texas campaign and served as deputy secretary of defense under both Nixon and Ford. For all his wealth and stature, however, he was a stranger to many Texas voters because of his years away in Washington, DC, and his lack of elective-office experience. Hutchison wasn't exactly a household name, but, at least in media circles, he was the most highly respected Republican in the state. He'd not only won raves for his legislative brilliance in the Texas House but had also received high marks for his two-year stewardship of the state GOP: helping the party reduce its chronic debt, creating a campaign reserve fund to assist Republican candidates, and pushing to get Southern states greater representation in the national party.

Even Ernest Angelo, who vaguely resented what he regarded as the pro-Ford tenor of Hutchison's GOP reign, ultimately came to respect the man's sense of fair play. "[Hutchison] is a gentleman, and one of the things he did as chairman was to put me in charge of creating a committee that would write the bylaws for the party," Angelo says. "He nearly got railroaded out of his chairmanship for doing that, because so many of the other members resented me having that position. So Ray was pretty straight about it all."

Hutchison's place in the GOP firmament was so solid that when Ray Barnhart challenged him for the state chairmanship in September 1976, even the swelling ranks of Reaganites in the party couldn't swing the race for Barnhart. State senator Betty Andujar of Fort Worth, a GOP national committee member who was one of Reagan's most ardent supporters in 1976, actually favored Hutchison over Barnhart. She praised Hutchison for his leadership and said his public neutrality during the '76 primary battle should not be confused "with enmity." Barnhart got his chance a year later, however, when Hutchison decided to step aside as state chairman in order to run for governor. There had been calls for Hutchison to make that jump in the past, and he'd always been strangely reluctant. In December 1973, he announced that he was filing for the gubernatorial race, only to change his mind less than a month later.

Hutchison now describes his 1978 gubernatorial run as a campaign he never wanted to make. He says as state chairman he was "frantic" to get good GOP candidates for governor, and even approached Clements about it while Clements was still serving in the Ford administration. "He declined, he was not interested," Hutchison says. "Then later he changed his mind and I had already announced by that time. So he did run and I'm glad he did, because I could not have raised the money to beat [Democratic nominee] John Hill. It was awkward. There were a number of people who asked me to drop out, and in retrospect I probably should have."

Hutchison's gubernatorial campaign came during a turbu-
lent and acutely painful period in his life. A month before he
announced his candidacy, his eighteen-year-old son Bradley Ray
Hutchison shot and killed himself in the garage of his University
of Texas dormitory. Hutchison had gone through a divorce from
Bradley's mother, Mary, and was preparing to marry his former
state-legislative colleague Kay Bailey. Hutchison and Bailey married less than two months before the 1978 gubernatorial primary, a
period so busy for Hutchison that the morning after his Dallas wed-
ding he had to speak to a group of senior citizens in Corpus Christi.

Under the circumstances, it would be easy to understand
Hutchison feeling distraught and distracted during his campaign.
But if he was a reluctant candidate merely going through the
motions, you couldn't tell from the pit-bull aggression he unleashed
on Clements. Hutchison accused Clements of all manner of unethi-
cal and/or simply crass behavior: having his supporters slow-drive
by Hutchison's house (which also served as his headquarters) to
monitor his activities; using a government plane for a pleasure trip
to a Colorado ski resort; receiving federally guaranteed credit for
an affiliate of his drilling company while serving in the Defense
Department; having a campaign worker break into his own headquarters after hours, presumably to find out what information a
disgruntled former staffer had run off with; and, finally, "flaunting
his wealth across Texas."

Without question, Clements had infinitely more money than
Hutchison and outspent him by nearly twenty to one in their primary race. Hutchison, however, had a potentially big advantage of
his own, because his two-year stint as party chairman enabled him
to build the kind of personal connections that Clements couldn't
match. Many Reagan 76ers held a grudge against his perceived
handling of the Ford-Reagan race, but some, like Steve Munisteri,

didn't hesitate to join his cause. Even Ray Barnhart, the party's state chairman by this point, bit his tongue and avoided taking sides.

Reagan clearly preferred Clements but chose to maintain a public neutrality. Clements, never celebrated for his discretion, couldn't contain himself and started publicly hinting that he had Reagan's backing. In response, Reagan sent a letter to Barnhart attempting to clear up the mess. (Clements made a similar faux pas with Tower, telling a Galveston audience: "Sen. John Tower has authorized me to say I would be worth 200,000 votes to him [in the general election]." Tower quickly authorized his campaign manager to deny Clements's claim.)

Clements was so eager to win the love of the hard-right Reagan crowd that he shamelessly reversed himself on the Panama Canal Treaty that he'd worked to make a reality under Ford. During the primary campaign, he sent out a statewide pseudo-newspaper mailing with a banner headline proclaiming, "Bill Clements: 'No on Panama.'"[75]

Clements also personally called Barbara Staff, Reagan's 1976 state tri-chairman, to ask if she'd work full-time on his campaign, and she agreed. "I knew that they were using my connections with the Reagan people, but that was okay, because Bill Clements was a good old guy," Staff says.

Clements and George Bush were old friends with a shared history in the oil business. Clements's position at the Pentagon had come at least partly because Bush made Nixon aware of him. Because both men had spent years outside of Texas working for Nixon and Ford, they were both scrambling to reconnect with the fast-changing political dynamics in their home state. In the '60s and early '70s, Bush had been the poster child for hard-luck Texas Republicans who couldn't break the Democratic Party's stranglehold. After failing in two tries for the US Senate, he got around the party's ultra-low glass ceiling by rising through appointed positions. He'd served as United Nations ambassador and chairman of the Republican National Committee under Nixon, and liaison to China and CIA director under Ford.

A Clements win would give Bush a valuable ally as he plotted out his 1980 presidential campaign and would be an early show of strength against Connally, who was also gearing up for a presidential run and was particularly close to Hutchison. (Hutchison had personally enlisted Connally in 1976 to serve as Texas chairman of Gerald Ford's general-election campaign.) In typical Connally fashion, however, Big John sensed that Hutchison's campaign was floundering, and he didn't want to get saddled with a loser. He opted to remain neutral but openly wished that Hutchison would pull out of the race and run for lieutenant governor instead.

By the middle of 1978, it became obvious that the conservative crusade Reagan led two years earlier was reverberating across the country. Jimmy Carter's poll numbers were lackluster, high inflation was a major political preoccupation, and a grassroots taxpayer revolt seemed to be gaining steam. In California, voters passed a controversial initiative called Proposition 13, which immediately slashed property taxes in the state by almost 60 percent. At least thirty states had citizens' groups working with legislators to amend state constitutions in order to put caps on government spending. Even in Jeff Bell's Senate race against Bill Bradley in New Jersey, where the demographics clearly favored the Democrat, Bell was able to pressure Bradley into supporting the Kemp-Roth tax bill before Congress at the time, which proposed major income tax cuts as a remedy for the nation's faltering economy.

In Texas, with the political climate turning inclement for Democrats, five veteran Democratic congressmen decided to retire at the same time. One of those Democrats was West Texas institution George Mahon, who had served in Congress for forty-four consecutive years and chaired the House's powerful Appropriations Committee. West Texas Republicans saw Mahon's retirement as a golden opportunity to pick up a congressional seat. The opening spurred George W. Bush, the thirty-one-year-old son of George H. W. Bush, to carry on the family tradition by making his first political run. And while Reagan chose not to get in the middle of a Republican fight when it came to Clements and Hutchison, he showed no such trepidation over a race involving George Bush's son.

In the primary, Bush was pitted against Jim Reese, a stockbroker and former mayor of Odessa. Ernest Angelo, whose home base of Midland was only a few miles from Odessa, liked Bush but stayed neutral in the primary, explaining, "because Jim Reese and I had been really good friends." Before long, the congressional primary race became a de facto battleground for the looming 1980 Reagan-Bush presidential contest. Reagan sent a letter of endorsement to Reese, which Reese dutifully mass-mailed to Republicans in the district. Bush initially tried to minimize the impact of the letter by saying it was not a true endorsement, but simply an expression of "best wishes."

In addition, Reagan's California-based political action committee, Citizens for the Republic, contributed $3,000 to Reese's campaign. Utah senator Orrin Hatch, a Reagan friend and supporter, also sent an endorsement letter to Reese, even though he'd never met the former Odessa mayor.[76] Reagan's effort to help Reese was something "which the Bush family resented for a long time," according to Angelo.

After Bush beat Reese in the runoff, Angelo assisted him as an "unofficial adviser" in the fall campaign against Kent Hance, a state senator from Lubbock. Hance portrayed Bush as a New England child of privilege with dubious Texas roots, and Bush allowed that image to stick. "George was running what I call a 'nice-guy campaign,'" Angelo says. "I told him personally that there was no way that we were in a position yet where Republicans could out-nice-guy a Democrat candidate and win."

"I had a lot of the Reagan people helping me," Hance says.

> They could see that for the 1980 presidential campaign it was going to be Bush vs. Reagan. And they didn't want another Bush to have a victory that might help his dad. I had a district that had seventeen counties and I carried fourteen. But out of those seventeen, I had already been representing thirteen of them for four years. I knew 'em, they knew me. So I had a great advantage over Bush. We tried to portray him as an outsider, and we defined him as an outsider. We're friends now, and he's told me since that he made the determination after that race was over: "Never let someone define who you are. You define who you are."

George W. Bush never lost another election.

In the '78 gubernatorial primary, Clements blew out Hutchison by a margin that astounded even his most optimistic supporters. In a race that many had initially expected Hutchison to win by a comfortable margin, Clements received 115,345 votes (75 percent) to only 38,268 (24 percent) for Hutchison.

Angelo contends that Hutchison's perceived support for Ford in the 1976 presidential primary did him no favors against Clements. "Clements had all the firepower to win the gubernatorial primary, so even if Ray had not been hurt in '76, he probably wouldn't have been able to win it," Angelo says. "But if he'd been a Reagan guy, he might have given Bill a pretty good run for it."

That fall, Clements shocked Democratic nominee John Hill in a tight race to become the first Republican governor in Texas since Reconstruction. In some ways, Clements's win was a fortuitous one-off for the Texas GOP. Clements was a forerunner of the wealthy self-funding politician, and his outrageously deep pockets solved the Republican Party's perennial problem of running out of money in the crucial final weeks of gubernatorial campaigns. Also, the 1978 turnout was remarkably low, which benefited Clements, the candidate with the narrower base.

But many Republican activists say it was no coincidence that only two years after Reagan elevated the Texas GOP to a new prominence in state politics, the party managed to break its long gubernatorial drought. "Without that '76 campaign that brought new people into political activism, I don't think Clements would have won the governorship, because it was a close race," Steve Heinrich says. Staff agrees, saying "Reagan's 1976 win pushed Clements right over the edge."

Clements's candidacy even brought Reagan and Ford together, albeit for a single night, as the former president and his 1976 challenger appeared at a $1,000-a-plate Dallas fundraiser for Clements on September 12, 1978. Predictably, Reagan framed Clements's campaign as part of a larger struggle for individual freedom, while Ford simply praised the managerial competence Clements displayed in the Defense Department. "If you elect Bill Clements," Reagan said, "you would fire a shot heard across this country, just like Proposition 13 was."[77]

Both Reagan and Ford coveted the 1980 presidential nomination, but Ford, seeing himself as the GOP's ranking elder statesman, wanted his party to call on him. It never happened. Reagan, after enduring an early upset victory by Bush in the Iowa caucus, took control of the Republican primary campaign. Connally put all his stock in a dubious Southern strategy and withdrew from the race after a distant second-place finish in South Carolina. He put fourteen months of work into the campaign, spent more than $10 million, and earned one delegate for his trouble. In his classic fashion, he quickly endorsed Reagan, the obvious front-runner, rather than his fellow Texan George Bush.

The 1980 race was Connally's last gasp as a major figure in American politics. He subsequently concentrated on a series of high-risk oil and real-estate ventures with former Democratic lieutenant governor Ben Barnes, and in 1987 he declared bankruptcy after disclosing that he had debts of more than $93 million. To pay off the debt, he and his wife Nellie auctioned off most of their possessions.

The following year, Connally continued to be a thorn in Bush's side by endorsing Bob Dole over Bush for the 1988 GOP presidential nomination. When Connally died in 1993 of pulmonary fibrosis, Bush issued a terse but complimentary remembrance, calling him "one of the great governors of Texas," and adding, "He represented his state and nation with distinction." Nixon's wife Pat was dying of lung cancer at the time and passed away a week after Connally. But Nixon, in a final show of admiration for the man he wanted to be his successor, left her side to fly to Austin for Connally's funeral.

Angelo, who viewed Connally with distrust during the '76 campaign, says he later came to respect the way Big John handled adversity. "He had a pretty good campaign debt when he endorsed Reagan, and I think they gave some assurance that they would try to help him a little bit, but he didn't push them hard on it or anything," Angelo says. "And when he got into financial trouble with Ben Barnes, he sold off a huge amount of his personal stuff, which he didn't have to do."

Reagan easily locked up the 1980 presidential nomination that summer at the Republican National Convention and, after a brief convention-week flirtation with Ford, settled on Bush as his running mate. That November, the Reagan-Bush team sailed to a land-slide victory over Carter, and the GOP gained control of the US Senate for the first time in twenty-six years. Ernest Angelo served as Reagan's Texas campaign manager that fall. Ray Barnhart had been appointed by Clements in 1979 to be a state highway com-missioner, a move that served two key purposes: It gave the cash-starved Barnhart a steady income, and it gave Clements a chance to move the ever-thorny Barnhart out of a leadership role in the GOP. Two years later, Reagan, in one of his first acts as president, rewarded Barnhart for his zealous campaign work by naming him administrator of the Federal Highway Administration, a position he held for six years.

As Reagan stood at the podium at the 1980 Republican National Convention in Detroit, waiting for the standing ovation to die down so he could begin his acceptance speech, a familiar chant filled the room.

"Viva!"

"Olé!"

"Viva!"

"Olé!"

As they had done four years earlier, the Texas and California delegations were shouting across the arena floor at each other, but not, as in 1976, to mischievously disrupt a convention that had turned away their candidate. This time, the "Reagan cheer," as Ernest Angelo called it, was pure cathartic celebration. The party they had once tried to upend now belonged to them.

CHAPTER 16

OIL, WATER, AND TEA

Rick Perry likes to say that he never met a Republican until he served in the air force in the mid-'70s. While that claim seems a tad hyperbolic (is it really plausible that in four years at Texas A&M University, a reliably conservative campus dominated at the time by its military corps of cadets, Perry never crossed paths with a single GOP supporter?), it conveys the political climate in which Perry came of age.

That climate changed so radically in the twenty-five years between the Reagan-Ford clash and the day Perry first took the oath of office as governor that it afforded him a level of power no other Texas Republican governor has ever enjoyed.

While the country has grown accustomed to the idea of Texas Republicans seeking the presidency, Perry is something the nation hasn't seen before. He's the first "Don't Mess with Texas" candidate, a Lone Star exceptionalist who unabashedly talks about wanting to remake the nation in the image of his beloved home state.

By comparison, George W. Bush—his gubernatorial predecessor, and the politician to whom he's most often compared—was a model of humility. Bush became defined as president by his bullheaded unwillingness to admit mistakes, but his tenure as governor was marked by bipartisanship, by his willingness to work with Lt. Gov. Bob Bullock and the legislature's Democratic majority. As a presidential candidate in 2000, he stood out largely because he advocated a "humble" foreign policy and described himself as a "compassionate conservative."

It's hard to imagine those words coming out of Rick Perry's mouth, but then again, unlike that of Bush, his gubernatorial tenure hasn't necessarily demanded an ability to play well with others. Less than two years into his administration, his party secured control of the legislature, and by 2011, the GOP had an overwhelming 101–49 supermajority in the Texas House. So it's easy to see that Perry's ever-present cockiness is as much a reflection of the GOP-dominated era in which he has governed as it is his own supreme confidence in his power to charm. The days of Texas Republicans practicing the fine art of cautious legislative counterpunching are gone, and Perry is basking in the changes that Reagan ushered in with the '76 primary.

Perry's uncompromising style reached its zenith during the state's heated 2011 legislative session. Despite anguished complaints from outnumbered Democrats, Perry successfully urged the passage of the following legislation: a requirement that sonograms be administered to women before they can have an abortion; the defunding of Planned Parenthood; cuts of $4 billion in public-education funding; and the requirement of identification cards for all voters.

Perry is the longest-serving governor in Texas history, but his vote-getting power was commonly questioned until the 2010 election. After all, he'd inherited the office in 2001 when George W. Bush relocated from the governor's mansion to the White House. In 2002, Perry beat a wealthy but politically green Laredo banker named Tony Sanchez. Four years later, he drew an uninspiring 39 percent of the vote in a four-candidate field that included songwriter-author Kinky Friedman. In 2010, however, Perry answered all questions about his political skills. To the surprise of many, he easily dismantled the campaign of popular US senator Kay Bailey Hutchison in the GOP primary. In November, he manhandled former Houston mayor Bill White, widely perceived as the Democratic Party's strongest gubernatorial nominee since Ann Richards left office in 1995.

Perry achieved this breakthrough by quickly attaching himself to the Tea Party movement and using that association to subtly rebrand himself. The man who has spent part of his governorship living in a $10,000-a-month, taxpayer-funded rental mansion, and who once embraced a $200 billion transportation network involving the eminent-domain takeover of thousands of acres of private land, is now a mad-as-hell, fed-up, states'-rights champion. That image shift has enhanced Perry's stature with grassroots Republicans and Tea Party activists around the country, but there is a sense that, unlike Reagan, Perry is piggybacking on a movement rather than leading it.

The Tea Party movement consciously flexed its muscle at the 2010 Texas State Republican Convention in Dallas, a Perry coronation party that also featured the emergence of a key link to the Reagan '76 campaign.

As delegates entered the Dallas Convention Center, they were instantly greeted by earnest teenagers handing out flyers in support of Steve Munisteri's candidacy for state party chairman. Munisteri's teen supporters were members of the Young Conservatives of Texas, an organization he'd helped to create three decades earlier, and the flyers included a photo of a young Munisteri proudly standing with Ronald Reagan. As Munisteri attempted to unseat incumbent Cathie Adams, an establishment Republican with limited grassroots appeal, his message was obvious, if unstated: Just as Reagan had taken the party away from a bloodless party establishment in 1976, Munisteri could do the same in 2010. Who better to run the party, the argument went, than someone who represented a bridge to the icon who had motivated many Texas Republicans to join the party in the first place? Since his days as a high-school volunteer at Reagan's Houston headquarters, Munisteri had gone on to a law career and a stint as a boxing promoter, but his fascination with Republican politics continued to drive him, as it did when he was a fourteen-year-old block-walker for Nixon and Tower.

The party Munisteri took over in 2010 was bigger than any Texas Republican could have imagined in 1976, but like the '76 incarnation of the party, it was grappling with the uncompromising force of a new group of ultraconservative ideologues. Tucked away in the back of the convention center's exhibit hall, the Tea Party Patriots of Texas, a coalition of the state's various Tea Party groups, held court. To find them, you had to navigate your way through a maze of commerce and ideology, including John Birch Society DVDs, T-shirts promoting guitarist/professional carnivore Ted Nugent for president in 2012, a magnetic therapy jewelry booth, and campaign buttons proclaiming "Hot Chicks Vote Republican."

Once you got close to the Tea Party booth, however, there was no mistaking it, because it was the only place where you could find a giant vinyl banner with thousands of signatures calling for a balanced-budget amendment to the US Constitution.

In a way, the Tea Party movement, with its "Don't tread on me" mantra, is just a looser, twenty-first-century version of the Reagan 76ers, but there is a crucial difference: Reagan's loyalists were united by their allegiance to one man, and, whatever their frustrations with the GOP, they stayed in line because they understood Reagan's commitment to the party. The Tea Party movement is united by an idea, not an individual, and while most of its members have roots in the Republican Party, they wouldn't hesitate to ditch the party organization if it failed to comply with their agenda. Felicia Cravens, founder of the Houston Tea Party, put it this way: "We train people to sign up as precinct chairs because that's the best way within the two-party system to get their voices heard. But we should be independent enough to stand outside the party and criticize what we don't like."

Josh McDowell, a technical writer from San Antonio who once worked as a TV weatherman, makes the strongest case for the Tea Party movement as modern-day Reagan 76ers. "We are the outsiders trying to push in," he says, sounding very much like Reagan's supporters during the campaign to unseat Ford. "And outsiders tend to have more energy in American politics anyway."

McDowell, like Munisteri, is a veteran of the 1976 Reagan-Ford clash. At that time McDowell lived in Washington, DC, where his father worked as a writer for *National Geographic*. James Baker offered the eighteen-year-old McDowell a job at Ford headquarters, handling a wide array of campaign grunt work. McDowell's dominant memory of the experience is watching Baker, a man who always projected the cool reserve of an expert poker player, literally work himself into a state of stomach-churning anxiety. "As the campaign wore on, Baker ate more and more Maalox," McDowell says. "I even delivered a case of Maalox to his office. This was a man who sweated the details."

The Republican Party, at both the national and state levels, has carefully courted the Tea Party movement in a way that it didn't with the Reagan 76ers insurgency. Party leaders at that time grumbled that Reagan diehards were extremists, prone to belligerence, and not necessarily true Republicans. But even as Republican pols publicly praise the Tea Party for bringing the GOP back to the cause of fiscal conservatism, some of these same Republicans privately complain that Tea Party members are an awkward fit among veteran, politically pragmatic Republicans. "You'll see them working at the campaign headquarters and they just don't mix with everybody else. It's like oil and water," says a Texas Republican legislator.

While Texas Republicans currently hold all twenty-nine statewide elected offices and overwhelming control over the Texas legislature, the state's demographic trends gnaw at them. Over the last decade, the state's population grew 21 percent, but the state's Latino population grew twice that fast, according to the 2010 Census. Latinos, who made up 32 percent of the state's population in 2000, now constitute 38 percent. Given the Democratic Party's history of success with Latino voters, some Texas Democrats predict that they'll be able to turn the state back from red to blue over the next decade.

The GOP rolled out its new strategy for reaching Latino voters at the state convention's Hispanic Leadership Breakfast. Rob Johnson, Rick Perry's 2010 gubernatorial campaign manager, said if the party could capture at least 40 percent of the Latino vote, it "would change the dynamics of Texas politics for a generation." Perry is mindful of how crucial the Latino vote is to his political prospects. He was able to fend off the 2002 general-election challenge from Sanchez largely because, even with Sanchez offering the possibility of the state's first Hispanic governor, Perry received 35 percent of the Latino vote.

In 2009, his appointment of Eva Guzman made her the first Latina ever to serve on the Texas Supreme Court. In 2010, he picked a Latino, Alejandro Garcia, to be his 2010 campaign press secretary. And whenever he's in South Texas, he doesn't hesitate to let voters know that his brother-in-law is a Latino. At the Hispanic Leadership Breakfast, Perry told the audience that Latinos offered the chance "to get a lot of new life" in the GOP. He said Republicans and Latinos had a "shared military background," a shared understanding of "the meaning of the church," and a shared dedication to family values. "This is the home of the Hispanic in America: The Republican Party," he said.

That message was strikingly similar to what Ronald Reagan said to Lionel Sosa when they met in September 1978 at the Dallas fundraiser for Bill Clements that brought Reagan and Ford together. Sosa, a San Antonio advertising consultant, had been hired earlier in the year by John Tower to put together a Latino-themed marketing strategy for Tower's reelection campaign. Tower had always worked harder than most Republicans to connect with the state's Latino voters, and, given the grudge that many Texas Reaganites carried against him after the '76 presidential primary, he sensed that his political survival depended on the Latino vote.

As a show of gratitude for the boost that Sosa's Spanish-language ads were providing him, Tower introduced Sosa to Reagan in Dallas. Sosa remembers that they only talked for a couple of minutes, but during their exchange, Reagan told him, "Hispanics are Republicans. They just don't know it yet." In 1980, Reagan hired Sosa to do for his presidential campaign what Sosa had done for Tower's Senate campaign, and Sosa has gone on to work for every Republican presidential nominee except for Bob Dole. When Sosa joined forces with Reagan, 8 percent of the Latino vote was the accepted ceiling for most Republican candidates. By 2004, however, Sosa was able to help George W. Bush bring in more than 40 percent.

Barack Obama turned that around for Democrats in 2008, and Sosa now frets that the GOP has ruptured its tentative bond with Latinos by supporting draconian immigration legislation such as Arizona's SB 1070, which enables local and state law enforcement officials to ask for proof of citizenship from passengers in a car that's been stopped for a traffic infraction. US representative Louie Gohmert, who has propagated the outlandish theory that the nation's birth-citizenship law could be abused by extremists hoping to raise terror babies whose citizenship rights would allow them to freely perpetrate acts of violence in this country, was introduced at the 2010 Texas state convention as "the conscience of Congress," and received one of the most enthusiastic greetings at the convention. Touting his immigration plan, which he said he modeled on Mexico's own tough immigration laws, Gohmert said, "Imitation of immigration is the highest form of flattery."

Initially, Perry carefully sidestepped the contentious Arizona law debate by saying such legislation wasn't a good fit for Texas, without actually condemning SB 1070. During the 2011 legislative session, however, he risked the ire of Latino voters by fast-tracking a divisive Voter ID bill and pushed for legislation that denied state funds to so-called sanctuary cities (the sanctuary cities bill failed to make it out of the legislature). Perry got a taste of the antipathy these bills aroused when he addressed the National Association of Latino Elected and Appointed Officials in San Antonio on June 23, 2011. As he commonly does, Perry touted the job-creating power of his state, but he was clearly taken aback by the icy reception his pep talk received.

The 2011 legislation was a tense, calculated six-month political gamble by Perry. He elected to solidify his credentials with both Tea Party activists and socially conservative fundamentalists, even if it cost him some Latino votes down the line. Perry has framed his presidential campaign as the product of a modern-day political draft: a campaign that he launched semi-reluctantly, and only because his country was begging him to answer the call. It's a narrative belied not only by his handling of the legislative session but also by the publication of his political manifesto, *Fed Up!*, within a week of his 2010 gubernatorial reelection.

Much as Perry attempts to cast himself in the role of a latter-day Reagan, some of his fellow Texans question whether his prickly exuberance—which has carried him to an unblemished 10–0 election record over the last twenty-eight years—will sell with a national audience. Nelson Wolff, a Democrat who served as a state senator and representative in the '70s, the mayor of San Antonio in the '90s, and is currently county judge for Bexar County, says, "I think Reagan had a way of reassuring people and making them feel very comfortable. I don't think Perry does that."

Ray Barnhart, the impassioned leader of Reagan's pivotal Texas breakthrough, is not among Perry's admirers. In addition, Barnhart, who is now retired and living in Ohio, sees no parallels between the man he loyally served and the current crop of GOP leaders. "I'm irritated with Perry," Barnhart says. "I mean, renting a place for $10,000 a month while the mansion gets fixed up, that's an absolute disgrace. I don't understand that. I always thought public service was public service, but I guess I'm naive. Reagan represented what Republicans should be advocating today. Unfortunately, we've got a bunch of flakes. I'm so fed up with the Republican Party, I haven't contributed a penny to them in thirty years."

Steve Munisteri maintains a more charitable view of the party he's served since his childhood. He sees the bitter Reagan-Ford battle as a struggle that helped the GOP grow, even as the party paradoxically became more narrowly ideological. "The liberal wing of the party is gone," Munisteri says. "The John Anderson, Nelson Rockefeller wing is completely gone. And even what some people would call the moderate wing of the party is just about gone. What you have left are different types of conservatives, and that's what we are."

The roots of that realignment can easily be traced to Reagan's stunning 1976 primary win in Texas. After that dramatic election night, conservative Democrats would never again feel as emotionally connected to their party as they once had, while moderate and liberal Republicans would never again feel as accepted in their party as they once had. Instantly, the old definitions seemed to lose some of their currency. "Conservative populist" was no longer synonymous with "Democrat," and "country club moderate" didn't automatically equate with "Republican." Rick Perry wouldn't realize it for more than a decade, but that night he became a Republican.

NOTES

INTRODUCTION

1. "Reagan's Startling Texas Landslide," *Time*, May 10, 1976.

2. Matt Lewis, "Texas Gov. Rick Perry to President Obama: Call Me," *Politics Daily*, July 26, 2010.

3. Paul Burka, "Right Place, Right Time," *Texas Monthly*, February 2010.

4. Richard Reeves, "The Last Reagan Campaign: Legacy," *Real Clear Politics*, February 5, 2011.

CHAPTER 1. TEXAS OR BUST

5. Matthew Dallek, *The Right Moment* (New York: Free Press, 2000), p. 203.

6. Jules Witcover, *Marathon: The Pursuit of the Presidency 1972–76* (New York: Viking Press, 1977), p. 37.

7. Witcover, *Marathon*, pp. 69–70.

8. "Ronald Reagan (1)," Box 25, Jerry Jones Files, Gerald R. Ford Library.

9. "DeBolt Subject File—Advertising," Box A11, President Ford Committee Records, Gerald R. Ford Library.

10. Pat Buchanan, "Connally Holding Catbird Seat," *San Antonio Express-News*, April 17, 1976.

11. Carolyn Barta, "Reagan Vows GOP Hierarchy Fight," *Dallas Morning News*, April 6, 1976.

CHAPTER 2. FAVOR FOR A FAVORITE SON

12. Al Reinert, *Texas Monthly*, December 1974, p. 72.

13. "The Ten Worst," *Texas Monthly*, July 1975.

14. Witcover, *Marathon*, p. 219.

15. "Bentsen Says He's Cleared of Campaign Charge," *Houston Chronicle*, April 15, 1976.

16. Bo Byers, "Bentsen Gets By Gramm 2–1," *Houston Chronicle*, May 2, 1976.

17. "Bentsen Is Keeping a Low Profile," *Houston Chronicle*, May 2, 1976.

18. Craig Hines, *Houston Chronicle*, May 1, 1976.

CHAPTER 3. THE TWO RAYS

19. Chandler Davidson, *Race and Class in Texas Politics* (Princeton, NJ: Princeton University Press, 1990), p. 214.

20. "Equal Time," *Texas Monthly*, May 1978.

CHAPTER 4. LYON'S GAMBIT

21. Craig Shirley, *Reagan's Revolution: The Untold Story of the Campaign That Started It All* (Nashville: Nelson Current, 2005), p. 185.

22. "Republicans: Reagan on the Offensive," *Time*, April 12, 1976.

CHAPTER 5. THE TRUTH SQUAD

23. Citizens for Reagan Records (CFRR), Texas, 1975–1976, Box/Folder 45: 9–10, Hoover Institution.

24. Carolyn Barta, "Reagan Blasts Dr. Kissinger," *Dallas Morning News*, April 7, 1976.

25. Witcover, *Marathon*, p. 418.

26. George Kuempel, "Reagan in Austin, Raps '2nd Best' U.S. Policy," *Houston Chronicle*, April 13, 1976.

27. Ibid.

28. Kemper Diehl, "Intimidation Charged," *San Antonio Express-News*, April 24, 1976.

29. CFRR, Texas, 1975–76, Box/Folder 45: 9-10, Hoover Institution.

30. Witcover, *Marathon*, p. 402.

CHAPTER 6. BIG JOHN'S QUANDARY

31. Buchanan, "Connally Holding Catbird Seat."

32. James Reston, "The Ghost at the Party," *New York Times*, August 15, 1976.

33. Barta, "Reagan Vows."

34. "Morton Didn't Intend to Snub Sen. Tower," *Dallas Morning News*, April 8, 1976.

35. Bob Tutt, "Reagan Says Ford Team May Have Made Illegal Job Offer to Connally," *Houston Chronicle*," April 16, 1976.

36. "Nancy Reagan Is Questioning Ford Administration Credibility," *Houston Chronicle*, April 22, 1976.

CHAPTER 7. ONE-PARTY STATE OF MIND

37. John R. Knaggs, *Two-Party Texas: The John Tower Era, 1961–64* (Austin: Eakin Press, 1986), p. 20.

38. "Texas Politics," *Firing Line*, January 23, 1973.

CHAPTER 8. THE GREAT TAMALE INCIDENT

39. Carolyn Barta, "Ford Says Texas Start Slow, but 'Underdogs' Often Winners," *Dallas Morning News*, April 10, 1976.

40. "Texas Politics," *Firing Line*, January 23, 1973.

41. Witcover, *Marathon*, p. 530.

42. Norman Baxter, "Ford Confident of Winning," *Houston Chronicle*, April 28, 1976.

43. "Ford Believes He's Underdog, Son Says Here," *San Antonio Express-News*, April 15, 1976.

44. Baxter, "Ford Confident."

CHAPTER 9. SENATOR IN EXILE

45. Griffin Smith Jr., "Little Big Man," *Texas Monthly*, January 1977.

46. Ibid.

47. Ibid.

48. Barbara Strong, "Tower Says If Reagan Can't Muster 75% He Should Quit," *Dallas Morning News*, April 8, 1976.

49. Ibid.

CHAPTER 10. RON PAUL'S GOLD STANDARD

50. "Republican Men's Club Advised to Proclaim Their Philosophy," *Dallas Morning News*, July 18, 1976.

51. "Paul's Bill May Prove Adage 'Money Talks," *Dallas Morning News*, May 25, 1979.

CHAPTER 11. STRETCH DRIVE

52. Louis Harris, "Ford Widens His Lead," *San Antonio Express-News*, April 29, 1976.

53. "Ford Charges Reagan with Superficiality," *Houston Chronicle*, April 27, 1976.

54. Harris, "Ford Widens His Lead."

55. Craig Smyser, "Reagan Says Recent Ford Attacks Are 'Intemperate,' Distort Positions," *Houston Chronicle*, April 30, 1976.

56. Vickie Davidson, "Nancy Follows Betty to S.A.," *San Antonio Express-News*, April 22, 1976.

57. "Wives Campaign in Austin," *San Antonio Express-News*, August 23, 1976.

58. Kemper Diehl, "Reagan Fan Says Ford Can't Win," *San Antonio Express-News*, April 29, 1976.

59. Craig Smyser, "Reagan Urges Dem Crossover Vote," *Houston Chronicle*, May 1, 1976.

60. James Sterba, "Ford Believed to Have Cut Reagan's Strength in Texas," *New York Times*, May 1, 1976.

61. "Reagan Path Looks Familiar to Goldwater," *Dallas Morning News*, May 3, 1976.

62. "Marsh, 1976–77 (2)," Box 30, James Connor Files, Gerald R. Ford Library.

63. "Ronald Reagan (2)," Box 25, Jerry Jones Files, Gerald R. Ford Library.

CHAPTER 12. A NEW AND INTRANSIGENT REGIME

64. Carolyn Barta, "Harmony State GOP Convention Goal," *Dallas Morning News*, June 19, 1976.

65. "Together We Could Have," *Texas Monthly*, August 1976.

66. Robert Baskin, "Will It Be a Gunfight at the GOP Corral?" *Dallas Morning News*, June 19, 1976.

67. "GOP Attacks Carter, Platform," *Dallas Morning News*, June 20, 1976.

68. "Conservatives Walk Out," *Dallas Morning News*, June 20, 1976.

CHAPTER 13. KANSAS CITY DREAMING

69. "No Love Lost between Texans, Betty Ford," *Dallas Morning News*, August 19, 1976.

70. "Jack Apologizes for Confetti Toss," *Denton Record-Chronicle*, August 19, 1976.

71. Tony Orlando with Patsi Bale Cox, *Halfway to Paradise* (New York: St. Martin's, 2002), p. 179.

72. "No Love Lost."

73. Robert Baskin, "GOP Will Need Strange Crowd," *Dallas Morning News*, August 19, 1976.

CHAPTER 14. WHAT IF?

74. Richard Dunham, "Reagan Shaped Today's State GOP," *Houston Chronicle*, February 6, 2011.

CHAPTER 15. STANDING IN THE SHADOWS

75. Carolyn Barta, "Reaganites Hold Key," *Dallas Morning News*, March 6, 1978.

76. "W. Texas Runoff Seen as Test of Muscle for Reagan, Bush," *Dallas Morning News*, June 3, 1978.

77. "GOP 'Stars' Meet in Dallas," *Dallas Morning News*, September 13, 1978.

ACKNOWLEDGMENTS

When I started working on this book in the summer of 2010, I was quickly gratified to find that most of the participants in the 1976 Texas presidential primary were eager to tell their stories, largely because they've long sensed that they were part of a pivotal moment in American politics. I am thankful to all of them for sharing their time and their recollections with me. In particular, I'd like to thank Mark Elam, Ernest Angelo, Ray Barnhart, Ron Paul, Steve Munisteri, Steve Heinrich, Polly Sowell, Shirley Green, Ray Hutchison, Steve Bartlett, Barbara Staff, Jim Lunz, Jeff Bell, Kent Hance, A. R. "Babe" Schwartz, Lila Cockrell, Van Archer, M. Stanton Evans, Nelson Wolff, Arthur Troilo, Bill Hobby, and Josh McDowell.

I'd also like to express my appreciation to Nancy Mirshah at the Gerald R. Ford Presidential Library, the staff of the Hoover Institution, and Jenny Fichmann for their patience and invaluable research assistance.

Finally, I'd like to thank the following people for their much-appreciated personal support and encouragement: Greg Jefferson, Elaine Wolff, Mary Ann Rios, Tom Payton, Sarah Nawrocki, Barbara Ras, Christi Stanforth, and Barbara Collins Rosenberg. Above all, I'd like to thank my family: my parents, G. G. and Josefina Garcia; my sisters, Rosa Cady and Josie Garcia; my wonderful wife, Elda Silva; and our beloved daughter, Olivia Garcia.

INDEX

GILBERT GARCIA, a native of Brownsville, Texas, is an award-winning reporter who has been recognized for his writing on politics, sports, music, and religion. He has worked for the *San Antonio Express-News*, *Phoenix New Times*, *Dallas Observer*, *San Antonio Light*, and *San Antonio Current*, and his work has also been published in *Salon* and the *Best Music Writing 2001* anthology. He currently writes for the online publication *Plaza de Armas TX*. He lives in San Antonio, Texas, with his wife, Elda, and daughter, Olivia.